Living Sacrifices

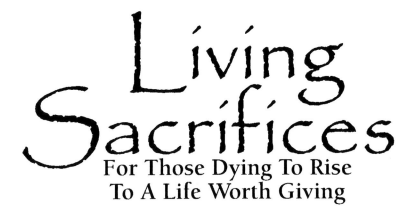

Living Sacrifices

For Those Dying To Rise
To A Life Worth Giving

James Haywood Rolling, Jr.

Pleasant Word
A Division of WINEPRESS PUBLISHING

Printed in the United States of America

Packaged by Pleasant Word, a division of WinePress Publishing, PO Box 428, Enumclaw, WA 98022. The views expressed or implied in this work do not necessarily reflect those of Pleasant Word, a division of WinePress Publishing. Ultimate design, content, and editorial accuracy of this work are the responsibilities of the author.

ISBN 1-57921-522-X
Library of Congress Catalog Card Number: 2002115098

Dedication

To all those who struggle and sacrifice daily
to give the best of themselves
to the many they love . . .

Life that is worth the giving!

Acknowledgments

- Thanks to God for making use of the life He has given me.
- Thanks to my wife, Me'Shae, for imparting to me her sense of order and for pardoning me for so many hours over the past few years spent sitting in front of a computer instead of by her side.
- Thanks to my mother, Sylvia, for passing on to me the gifts of resolve, persistence, and quiet strength.
- Thanks to my father, Jim, who passed away on July 8, 2002, for passing on to me the inheritance of every artistic gift I possess.
- Thanks to my friend and long distance editor, Steve Lyons, a true servant, and a craftsman with words. May he be blessed for the year he gave to the task of fine-tuning this document, helping me to say what I wanted to say, helping me to discard what was unclear. I trust his voice as much as my own.
- Thanks to my friend Jacqueline Oliver for her suggestions, proof-reading, and page-by-page encouragements, supporting me in any way she could.
- Thanks to my brothers-in-Christ, Gene Morris and Sam Rivera, and others who upheld my confidence by taking the time to read the manuscript as it was still being formed.

- Thanks to my cousin Stephanie and my sister Angie for helping to provide a way.
- Thanks to brother Nick Cymbala, the late father of my senior pastor, Jim Cymbala, for the inspiration for Chapter Twelve.
- Thanks to The Brooklyn Tabernacle's Christian Education Department for allowing me to work as a teacher and indirectly providing the soil for so many fertile ideas.
- Thanks to my senior pastor Jim Cymbala for being my faithful, loving shepherd. So many of his sermons are right here in these pages.
- Thanks to my ministry leader, Carol Cymbala, for her quiet and powerful faith, pushing us all to greater excellence.

As the rain and the snow come down from heaven, and do not return to it without watering the earth and making it bud and flourish, so that it yields seed for the sower and bread for the eater, so is my word that goes out from my mouth. It will not return to me empty, but will accomplish what I desire and achieve the purpose for which I sent it.

The Bible (Isaiah 55:10,11)

Contents

Preface

"... in view of God's mercy, offer your bodies as living sacrifices, holy and pleasing to God—which is your spiritual worship. Do not conform any longer to the pattern of this world, but be transformed by the renewing of your mind."

The Bible (Romans 12:1,2)

You and I are taught from youth to look out for number one. We're warned, "If we don't take care of ourselves, no one else is going to." A common flag bearing the phrase "PROTECT OUR NATIONAL INTERESTS, BY ANY MEANS NECESSARY" is flown proudly above every nation in the world today. A sign that reads "I DESERVE THE BEST" is held high above the heads of individuals everywhere.

I raise no complaint about any of this, for good reason. I don't disagree that we should all do the most we can for ourselves. Everyone wants the best out of life. Most of us might even agree that perhaps the best life has to offer us is the opportunity to love and to be loved by others. In fact, there are volumes of evidence to show that the most necessary ingredient for sustaining physical and mental health living is <u>tender</u> <u>loving</u> <u>care</u>.

Consider the tragic effects the absence of love has on anyone's life. It might be the trembling infant abandoned at birth, screaming weakly from a hospital crib to be held in anyone's arms; or the elderly gentleman abandoned by his children, daydreaming in a nursing home bed about disassociated scraps of memory. Whatever the stage of life, the most crucial aspect of taking care of number one is *"the tender loving care of number one."* Feeling loved. Loving yourself. Holding a place of importance.

As an introduction to the book **Living Sacrifices**, I would like to present the simple paradox that arises when we fully consider the highest form that love of self takes. If I believe my priority should be to "look out for number one," I must devote the majority of my time, energy, and effort to serving my own needs. Yet in doing just so, I at the same time sabotage any possibility of that time, energy, and effort working out their unspoken goal: TO BE ACKNOWLEDGED BY OTHERS AS A PERSON OF IMPORTANCE.

As an individual, I am but a fraction of all that the human race is; I am just a part of what we all are as a whole. If I invest my life into myself first and foremost with a self-centered agenda, the rest of the human race misses out on whatever I accumulate to my private gain. By giving the best of my time, energy, and effort scraping together all that I can for personal gain alone, the result will be a weakening—eventually, a rupturing—of the ties that bind me to the whole.

A painful detachment then occurs. I am left unimportant to the same humanity I cut off! Thus, I am left diminished. I am left as the sole measure of my significance. I am left as the center of my own amputated existence. I am left without vital connection to a vast humanity—or my own loved ones.

I was only twelve years old when I started high school. I had skipped seventh grade and had a December birthday, so I was very much out of my peer group as I started at the High School of Art and Design in New York City. And I was also quite naive.

By that time I was already a dedicated loner. I had plenty of practice at navigating the world in isolation. I had a short lifetime of experience living out this admittedly awkward social concept—in my very own home. Even though I lived in a home with my parents, two brothers, one sister, and at times a cat, my ties to their living were quite severed. And I wanted it that way.

I didn't want to be close. I preferred privacy. I neither had a dear friend, nor knew how to make one. Even if I had such a friend I wouldn't have mentioned him to my family. I wasn't mean or angry—I was simply detached. All throughout grade school, I took no part in extracurricular activities and I had no popularity. I was pretty much limited to hearing my name called when my teacher called attendance . . . or when I won some sort of award.

I won lots of awards. But they were *mine*. I don't remember running home to share them to my family. I remember collecting these awards in a shoebox in one of my dresser drawers. For some reason I was proud in that only I knew they were there.

Sometimes, before my adolescent years, the family would gather to watch something funny on the T.V. The laughter would attract me. I'd leave my bedroom and tiptoe down the hallway. But I would stop in the shadow just outside the living room doorway. From that vantage point, I could see little more than half the T.V. screen at best. But I wouldn't enter the living room when it was full of laughter. It wasn't a comfortable place for me to be. Eventually one of my parents would notice me in the shadows, muffling my giggles, working very hard to contain myself, trying to be unseen. My father usually asked me to join everyone, but I always declined. Sometimes I'd watch a whole movie just like that, standing with my neck craned in the hallway corner just outside the living room doorway. That strange habit went on for years.

On bright Christmas mornings, I avoided all laughter and commotion. At some calculated point in time, when I knew the early morning excitement had surely died down, I marched determinedly into that living room, collected every present with my name on it, tossed out each "thank you" I knew I owed, and without demonstration walked with this armful—with not a wrapping removed—into the solitude of my bedroom.

I was always relieved when I got behind my closed door. There I would relax and open my gifts where I could experience them alone. It never occurred to me that the family who gave me those gifts might get some pleasure from seeing the suppressed smile that might flicker across my face if I'd unwrapped my presents along with everyone else. And I was always polite enough to thank them again later once I knew what new things I owned.

Every once in a while, in high school, I heard the charge that so-and-so said I was conceited. I was cut to the core. My denial of such accusations was vehement and my defense was sincere. I used logic in response. "I don't consider myself better than anyone else so I can *never, ever* be called conceited." I was very proud to be able to say this of myself.

Boy, was I conceited!

I had some imagination about who I thought I was, didn't I? Ironically, I was devoted to my self and my own opinions. By doing so, there was no other perspective on my life that I deemed necessary to discover. I was devoted to my own point of view; I saw myself as usually right while others were usually wrong. It's the kind of detachment that prevents intimate connections with the many who might otherwise have claimed me as an asset to their living.

Lets get to the bottom of something. What is the real point of the "look-out-for-number-one" philosophy? The answer is within the phrase itself—the need to know that I am acknowledged as important . . . *numero uno* to at least *some*one. For too many of us, we become our own faithfully applauding 'someone.' Self-important individuals fortunate enough to practice highly visible professions might even garner for themselves a fan club and offer to sell autographs or their personal belongings to the highest bidder. But it's all based on an incredibly desperate falsehood: a tale of amputated living masquerading as a legend of self-importance.

So now we arrive at the crux of our paradox: if I truly wish to be loved and acknowledged by others as an important individual in the world, then I must abandon the proud struggle to raise myself into a one-roomed tower above my neighbors' heads. Instead, I *must* come down and walk the same paths as my neighbors, dine at their tables, fling open my doors, and invite others to stay awhile. When what is mine is shared out so that strangers become my neighbors, what is theirs has reason to be shared with me. I then become doubly increased.

Therefore, the highest form of love for self is the sacrifice of investments solely into my own life—and instead investing into the OTHER lives that surround me. By making OTHER lives my priority, I deposit the best of me into living beings who deliver an compounded return from their increased lives back again into me!!

It is only when others are allowed close enough for an abundant exchange to pass between hearts, that "number one" is truly taken care of. To live without such exchanges is to live an insignificant existence, worthless to others.

In these pages I will argue that the reason men and women are driven by the desire to be considered first and foremost is that somehow we are all internally aware that our calling must be to live important lives. It is our capacity to love that informs us of this: we know there must be *some*thing we can add to others' lives! But we have a major problem here. **In spite of our highest aspirations, genuine personal sacrifice is still the hardest thing for humans to do!** Why is this? It is only through the act of offering our lives that the high calling of important living is ever achieved. Why then do we offer so little of ourselves?

We have just concluded that as we share the best of ourselves with others, at our own expense, we make a positive difference. And because we are embraced as a part of the lives of those who were once strangers, we are increased as well. So why are exchanges of the heart so begrudgingly given? Why is it so difficult to act with positive intentions toward everyone we have contact with? Why is it so easy to overlook that those whom nations honor as their heroes are those who sought the welfare of their fellow men and women above all else? Why is it so difficult for us to rise to a life worth giving even as we *ache* to shed our limitations and take our place in the heights? What's holding us down? What will lift us up?

In Chapter 1, *Living Sacrifices* reveals the folly of the great lies of humanity—the lie of self-importance, the lie of self-reliance, and the lie of self-indulgence—deceptions we believe will bring us pleasure and peace of mind.

Chapter 2 presents an examination of the waywardness of the United States which has pursued these great lies as inalienable rights.

In Chapter 3 our distorted behavior is presented as evidence of a terminal malady of the spirit. The proliferation of religious and self-help agendas is contrasted with hard questions of the direction our true help *must* come from.

Chapter 4 speaks of the need for a Savior and an extraordinarily special offer that has been extended to you and me.

In Part II of *Living Sacrifices*, the text seeks to illustrate the transformative power in compliance with God's extraordinary provision. In Chapter 5 we are presented with several new perspectives, all in parable form. One is directly from the text of the Bible, and others are from my point of view, from the Savior's point of view, and from the Creator's point of view, all serving to illustrate how all things change when an important life is abandoned or received. This chapter concludes with an invitation to be born-again into important living.

Chapter 6 examines what it takes to get in sync with the new vitality God provides as He carries us to a place of true importance within His scheme of things.

Chapter 7 looks closely at the intimacy created by prayer between a resourceful God and all those created in His image. This chapter concludes with observations on the power available upon request as we begin lives responsive to God's callings.

In Chapter 8 we begin studying the principles of humility, obedience, loving, and giving—and the bounty returned as a supernatural consequence of the initiative to serve others before self.

In Part III of *Living Sacrifices*, the text seeks to reveal the power and authority we have been granted to overcome evil with good. In Chapter 9 we will investigate the process of emptying self that we might be filled to a greater capacity by the fullness of the Holy Spirit. The chapter also reexamines the practice of fasting and the biblical references to the "gifts of the spirit" and the "fruits of the spirit."

Chapter 10 explores our military assignment in spiritual warfare against the adversary of God: our conscription into service; the declaration of war; the opponent's tactics; strategies for victory; our mighty fortress; our armor; our weapons; and our allies.

Chapter 11 defines the diplomatic office and responsibilities of an ambassador of God: protecting the vital interests of our kingdom; negotiating between our King and those not of His Kingdom; and ceremonial representation.

And finally, Chapter 12 is a carefully observed analysis our peculiar spiritual defect, our sin, which kills the body, the soul, and the spirit. This chapter draws the conclusion that this defect may be likened to an aberration in our genetic blueprint, never within the scope of our original design. In order for our salvation to be made complete, we must be conformed to the likeness of Jesus Christ who was miraculously and uniquely born without defect, the living image of God.

The search to be released from the deadly undertow of our personal interests will only be the start of the exciting adventure we can begin here. If not for yourself, begin the adventure for someone you want to love.

Part 1.

"...IN VIEW OF GOD'S MERCY..."

EXCESS

I have swallowed the glassy fruit of pride,
I'm softly sliced inside as
I indulge myself once more in my fatal addiction
I'm falling
swimming
ripping through my failing self-image
I vomit forth my tasteless visions
thick ego trips
pour forth from me
my SELF
my sweet significance
shouting:

power, power
mine all mine
keep off the private property!!!

Now oils of cool tranquility
anoint my god: My Inner Spirit.
I am bathed in rich self-certainty
as I unleash my earthly lusts
to sweep in liquid sheets across my eyes;
I applaud me for my self-manipulation.
and I embrace the feathery scented pillow now laid across my face
pressed against my face?
strapped tightly to my skull?! . . . I
cannot breathe! I . . .
cannot see!! I'm . . .
trapped inside . . .
I can't get out!!!
pray for me, I . . .
can't get free . . .

My God, I've murdered me . . .

Chapter 1

Fatal Living

He who lives with untruth lives in spiritual slavery.
Freedom is still the bonus we receive for knowing the truth.
(Dr. Martin Luther King, Jr.)

From my youth I reacted strongly against the capturing or caging of living things. I thought there was something wrong in it. Although I had a fascination with insects like ants and bees (often standing stooped over them in my front yard as a motionless observer), unlike other boys my age I would never capture one and take it home in a bottle. It didn't seem at all respectful to creatures I truly respected.

These feelings were cemented in my early teens when I went to visit the Central Park Zoo—before it was thankfully renovated to eliminate the crueler flaws in its concrete and bar design. But not before I saw something I've never forgotten. I watched as a large, beautiful cat, captured from the wild, paced back and forth in a black metal cage. The cage didn't seem any more than three times the animal's length from nose to tip of tail. The large animal was forced to wheel quickly and sharply because its strides carried it across the cage in a matter of seconds, and there was little maneuvering room for its bulk. But the pacing never paused.

I watched for half an hour and not once did the cat give a glance at the onlooking crowd. He didn't care about us. There was never a break in its pacing. The pattern of his nearly silent footfall, the vacant glaze in his eyes, these did not change once in that half hour. I watched and I became horrified, because as I watched I became certain that before me was a creature dulled into insanity by the ridiculousness of its confinement.

I wanted so badly to see that big cat set free. But at the time, and in my own way, I was as ridiculously confined as the cat. I'm sure the imprisonment of my own young mindset was once just as horrifying to behold. Before I would ever become an aid to anyone else's liberation, someone would eventually have to take hold and shake me free of the "insanity" of my own condition.

If you are not free—like a branch that sprouts from a vine is free to live a life of consistent growth, year after year stretching and extending itself to new lengths and new strengths, season by season multiplying its fruitfulness—then guess what? Something's severing the flow that is designed to keep you alive! Strangulation has a fatal conclusion. Anyone living in a condition that chokes off growth will die an untimely death.

The use of language here is intended to be bold, because we all need a firm understanding beneath our feet before a first step of exploration can ever be taken. For any who are willing to accept the challenges herein, the opportunity exists to be escorted onto a path of unimagined growth and adventure. However, the first steps in any walk of our lives will likely prove to be the most uncertain. Therefore, the first chapters of this book will seek to do nothing more than to map out some of the harsh territory within which too many of us find ourselves familiar.

Let's seek, then, to survey this familiar ground, so commonly traversed by wanderers like you and me—sheep bleating aimlessly into uncertain twilight. If only the truth were told, we might cross over to that land overflowing with milk and honey and a quality of land worth living upon.

THE LIE OF SELF-IMPORTANCE

The human spirit is a needy entity. From the depths of each of us, without exception, rises the basic impulse to somehow knit and bond with other individuals. This begins with our mother as we grow in her womb, extending later to our immediate family, and then to those we gather to ourselves as friends. With time and the proper effort, layers of intimate relationships develop.

These are multiplied many times over by the billions of people that inhabit the Earth, all of them overlapping each other with fewer degrees of separation than we may suppose. Your brother becomes my best friend . . . my distant cousin happens to be your new wife . . . your ancestors shared the language and resources of my culture. This is the common ground that binds the human community!

Our need for each other is no accident. If you or I were born and left abandoned on an empty field, without any others who could provide for our needs, we would not survive a week of our infancy. We were designed in need of some *other* to connect with; we were designed with needs only others can fulfill.

Nobel Prize laureate Martin Luther King, Jr., once wrote, **"We are caught in an inescapable network of mutuality, tied in a single garment of destiny. Whatever affects one directly affects all indirectly . . . ."**

If we choose to unravel our attachments to the whole of this grand, living tapestry, our importance to the whole human project vastly diminishes. Our place within the strength of the quilt is dangerously disconnected. Dangling threads also risk tearing away at the fabric of those closest to us. When we pull away from our common connections, we pull others away as well!

Isolation isn't part of the human design. Isolation leaves us unvalued and unclaimed, a swatch of leftover cloth swept up with the dustballs in the corner. I am suggesting here that our inborn desire to be considered important is correlated with our inborn need to be connected to others—**because it is only from others that we receive the affirmation that our life is truly important to them!!**

The ultimate value of a person, place, or thing is a function of the many who may find enough value there to grab hold of and weave into the masterpiece we call community. How absurd are those who insist on the lie that they individually . . . their race . . . their religion . . . their culture . . . or their nation, were born more important than any other! How destructive is the practice of a "mine first—your leftovers" mentality. How great is the insanity of those who unravel their place in the tapestry of human fellowship, removing their lives to that corner of the darkened room where one loses all sense of where in the world they might once have fit in.

THE LIE OF SELF-RELIANCE

I have nothing against inner resourcefulness or ingenuity—the ability to pull one's weight and adapt to new, unexpected situations. These are inarguably virtuous and admirable traits. Unfortunately, there also exists a ghastly attitude which couples together a pride in *"NOT NEEDING ANYBODY!"* with a stunning lack of awareness that we all are in fact totally interdependent!

We are clearly likewise dependent on nature's food chain, the clean water we ingest, and the very air we breathe. We are clearly likewise dependent upon the raw materials and resources produced by other communities who grow, refine, and then sell their products on the common market. We are likewise dependent upon the gravitational forces controlling the spin of our planet, our exposure to the sun, and the orbit of our entire galaxy through space. Although these truths stand self-evident, still we stand up straight and tall and proclaim our own independence!

What could we possibly be thinking? When we make our claims of independence, who do we believe we're independent from? Since our birth, we've been dependent on others. And for as long as we continue to need, for as long as we continue to want, we'll continue to be just as dependent. Yet, sometimes as a product of deliberate neglect, and at other times as a product of a very sick intent to injure, those nearest to us inflict such pain that we do cry in defensive agony, "I don't need you!" The callousness of others leads to the hardening of our own heart . . . which leads to the chafing away of the tender cords that were meant to tie all hearts together.

In the name of self-preservation, the doctrine of self-reliance has raided and robbed whole communities, exploited families, and diminished thriving societies. History speaks. From the self-reliant posturing fueling the most ancient clan warfare, through the self-reliant arrogance fueling the most recent government-sponsored genocide, harshness begets more pain, people claim the right of greater independence from each other, and communities and nations of the world are flung further apart.

All this is married to that ugly philosophy that just won't go away— the crude belief that "might makes right," and the updated revision, "the survival of the fittest." If you could hear the thoughts underneath the philosophy, don't be surprised if this is what you hear:

> "My brother is very different from me. That means his living is less important than mine since I am of number one importance. My importance is enough for me; I, therefore, do not need my brother. Since my ways must always supersede his, I must protect myself from him. So I will fight him and terrorize him, or I will conquer him and subject him to me. That way he cannot take my place. My prominence. I will prove him to be unnecessary and that makes me very happy."

THE LIE OF SELF-INDULGENCE

Of course, along with our self-important posturing and our self-reliant chest-beating comes the consequence of unquenchable self-indulgences.

Once we've convinced ourselves that we are destined for greatness, we have no choice but to feed the great appetites of self-importance . . . the need to acquire more and more material goods . . . more and more net worth . . . and more and more sensual pleasures of greater and greater strength with ever increasing regularity. We surround ourselves with things grand and flagrant, things rare and expensive, things of pomp and prestige, and things that tickle our curiosity. These are the new-age gods of our creation. They're the recipients of our time, our service, our passion, our pursuit, and our admiration.

These hungers grow with every new taste. With each taste, desires explode anew upon our tongues. Pangs fill our bellies. Often we'll even *take* what we want whether or not it belongs to another. Even the cutest, most innocent toddlers play this game. It's no secret; it's human nature:

> **"If I don't take it first, somebody else will."**
> **"You let me take it from you, so too bad . . . it's mine now."**

Our indulgences grow to become our entertainments, our obsessions, and our addictions. They help us occupy our time and overlook our pain. We'll mask the traumas and fears of everyday life by hiding in front of flashing televised images, amid myriad aisles of department store state-of-the-art things, behind walls of pulsing club music sound, and under the blankets of alcohol and drug-induced stupors. We stupefy ourselves against a reality that frightens us.

Yet we end up suffering anyway!

I believe that humankind has chosen to mutilate the garment of unity we were born to share with all other living beings. We have believed the lie of independence and have shorn away from the authentic reason for human communities—mutual support. Instead we've been making up reasons for living together as we go along. The needless repetition of acts of self-importance, self-reliance, and self-indulgence have afflicted every society history has recorded. That's why the words injustice, abuse, racism, slavery, tyranny, and genocide exist in the human language. In short, *we make incredibly harmful choices.* By our own acts we have been slowly pulling apart the great common tapestry of earthly creation. But the planet has its limits. Understood this way, even the increasing occurrence of natural disasters begins to make horrifying sense.

STOP AND THINK.

I will think about my place in the world.
Who am I attached to?
Who calls me out as important?
Who do I rely on?

I will identify the indulgences I have nurtured,
which have become the behaviors I'm now compelled to feed.

LIVE A LIFE WORTH GIVING.

SONGS OF TRANSGRESSION

Lift every voice and sing,
sing of the open sewers
that run where towns and cities once were raised.
Now our people lay caught in their own moral waste
which has with pestilence displaced
the promise of these fruited plains;
America is disgraced.

CHORUS: The stars are entombed in empty space,
        and the stripes have been stripped away.

Sing out to judgment's bloody flame,
washing from sea to shining sea
over purple mountains' majesty down to valleys in between,
swallowing our hearts in a toxic flood,
in the scalding rinse of a starving blaze,
in the spout of an aimless, shameless rage
reducing our loves to charcoal remains
made in the U.S.A.

CHORUS: We kill off all our deepest needs,
        and all that's left are the wasted days.

Turning 'round our partners like a springtime jamboree,
We, the naked, twirl and drown in the storm of a windy sea
unclothed of the glory our kind might have shared
gasping for the rare air that is no longer here—
that sweet breath of God that once whispered our names
yet was spurned in His offer to save and reclaim—
so that now all we taste is the salt of cold spray in our lungs
as we suck the briny stuff of our graves
and suffocate finally far under the waves
of fear that's eroding our lives.

CHORUS: Our living has been watered down,
        it's dribbling all away.

Let's celebrate the death of man!
Let's entertain ourselves in spite!
Let's watch the rising body count on network T.V. news tonight!
Let's crack the ringing doomsday bell!
Let's party till the break . . . of dawn . . .
No more. I can't go on like this . . .
The seventh seal's about to break . . .
The sun's on the horizon.
See!! The temperature is rising . . . the temperature is rising . . .

CHORUS: There's nothing left to say
        but that all we, like sheep, have gone astray.

My Country 'Tis Of Thee, Of Thee I Sing

"Go to this people and say, 'You will be ever hearing but never under-standing; you will be ever seeing but never perceiving.' For this people's heart has become calloused; they hardly hear with their ears, and they have closed their eyes. Otherwise they might see with their eyes, hear with their ears, understand with their hearts and turn and I would heal them."

(A quote from the New Testament book of Acts 28:26, 27)

When I was a child, I tended to stay away from playground swing sets. They disappointed me. I found them limiting. I discovered that the po-sition of the framework determined the direction of my swing. Trying to swing sideways or diagonally jerked me around annoyingly until the swing chains settled back into place. I realized that by sitting in a swing seat, I had to go in the direction it was designed to take me. I could only take so much of that kind of demand on the use of my time. It was usually only after a couple of unsatisfying minutes on a swing that I gave up on the idea, stabbed my feet into the ground, and stopped my momentum.

I remember how nice it felt to stop the ride and walk away in a direction the swing would never have taken me. Today I'm even more satisfied—I've taken an even greater departure from the ordinary swing of things.

Do we like the swing America has taken? Do you like where that swing has taken you? If you want a true picture of your personal standard of living, take a look at the community you call home, and the behavior of the people who surround you. Every society is the sum total of the individuals that constitute it. And its children will learn from birth to conform themselves to those around them who shape their surrounding environment.

In asking that we take a look at our America—without covering our eyes—we are open to see and understand our own societal machinations. A society perpetuates itself by a form of mass-manufacturing, stamp-cutting a common point of view for all who are willing to hop on board, and molding the ideological framework upon which the swing of an entire nation may be hinged.

"THE CRAVINGS OF THE SELFISH MAN"

Imagine, if you can, a place like this . . .

A place where men, women, and their children are given up by state and local governments to survive in city streets, collected into unsafe shelters, and stuffed into dangerous, vermin-infested hotel rooms for their "welfare."

A place where our elders (because of the "inconvenience" they begin to create) are consigned to nursing homes and institutions, doomed to the loneliest of kind of dying in which all the wisdom they have accumulated and love they have invested in their families is put to waste.

A place where those who are low-income community members are targeted to be overcharged in their little neighborhood convenience stores, despite their insufficient earnings, by the modern-day tax-sheltered franchises.

A place where our children are neglected before their birth and victimized afterward; where our innocents are viciously beaten, abused and broken in the hands of "parents and guardians;" where children promise to grow up more dysfunctional than the many thoughtless adults who are their role models.

A place that offers a bathhouse of sexuality and bloody low-budget cable broadcasts beamed into our family rooms as adolescent mind-candy or as action blockbusters, "slasher" flicks or "adult" films.

A place where the truth of our history is left untaught—that the Western Europeans who settled here and called themselves "Americans" possess this great land from shore to shore only because they conspired against the Native-American and Mexican nations, killing off the majority, and herding the survivors onto destitute reservations and into impoverished economic conditions.

A place where untold numbers of Africans died or were murdered in the chains of transport to these shores; where their African-American survivors and other peoples of color have for centuries been terrorized by threat of indiscriminate lynching or assassination or oppression based on racial biases and exclusion.

A place where the "crime" of a different walk or talk or appearance can be "punished" by a bashing or a stabbing or a torture at the hands of neighbors who deem themselves superior, but actually are just afraid.

A place where in any town or city or school building, random, irrational, spur-of-the-moment mass murder sprees are commonplace and out of control; where gangs, thugs, and idle middle-class youths roam the streets and graveyards like predators.

A place where the general public is denied full awareness of their government's covert actions against foreign governments . . . of the extent of their government's secret support of criminal authoritarian regimes . . . of arrogant acts of domestic surveillance, defying all rights to privacy . . . of corporate conspiracies, political imprisonments, false arrests, racial profiling, white-collar cover-ups, disavowed illegalities, all perpetrated in the name of "our national interests."

A place of self-destructive tendencies and neuroses: "panic attacks" and food disorders, obsessive-compulsive behaviors and irrational phobias, alcohol addictions, nicotine addictions, caffeine addictions, prescription-drug addictions, illegal-drug addictions . . . and even sexual addiction, feeding the epidemic spread of both disabling and lethal sexually-transmitted diseases.

A place where our animals are either unnaturally pampered, exploited, experimented upon, or locked up in zoos . . . or just plain driven to near extinction; a place where the land, sea, and sky are chemically polluted, radioactively poisoned, and shocked by the toxicity of a flash flood of human sewage.

But the place just described is not imagined—it is the United States of America. For over two centuries, this country has presented itself as a place of vast abundance. Full of life, liberty, and the pursuit of happiness. America works hard to put its best face forward . . . the haughty face worthy of "a leader among nations." But America has *two* faces—it is also a place of vast indulgences and violent indignities. Even when its founding fathers introduced America to the world as the model of religious and political freedom, many of those founding fathers owned and subjugated dark-skinned people like they were cattle.

"The Lust of His Eyes"

"I gotta have it!" This is a familiar phrase in the American language; after all, there's just so much of everything at our convenience. What is seen—what is then desired—is suddenly grasped, grabbed, and then clutched with a brief glow of satisfaction, until the next Cabbage Patch Doll or Tickle-Me Elmo hits the shelves. More, always more. Like the toddler who, upon noticing a small red ball in the corner of the living room, scrambles headlong toward the shiny object, snatches it up and raises the plunder as high above his large head as his short arms will allow and with a sudden cry defiantly proclaims, "**MINE!!!**" The fact that the ball obviously belongs to someone else in the house is irrelevant to the child; he has appropriated it and will *not* relinquish it until death . . . or a slap on the hand . . . brings parting! That is, of course, until the toddler glimpses the big black and white soccer ball through his sister's open closet door . . . for then the small red ball will be tossed in the toy box, and forgotten, as the little boy dashes again to satisfy the newest pangs of acquisition.

Above is an illustration of capitalism at work. Capitalism is the economic system upon which this nation was built. It's a simple ideology, a long-standing religion of far-reaching influence. Those who practice it do so in service to a trinity of gods—SELF, PRIVATE PROPERTY, and PERSONAL PROFIT MOTIVE. You see, capitalism preaches and dictates that a community's essential means of industry and production . . . its output . . . be owned not by the members of that community, but by a self-sufficient minority of individuals who, through the economic vitality drawn from their greater access to privately owned capital resources, employ other individuals to produce the maximum amount of labor for the minimum amount of wages that can possibly be paid. All in service to personal profit motive.

The employer, wrapped in his or her cloak of self-importance, sighs and justifies the imbalances of this situation. After all, aren't they the ones who started the business? Self-reliantly they bluster, aren't they the ones who are doing all the real work? Self-indulgently they say, shouldn't they be the ones to profit the most since they risk the most if the business ever fails? It's somehow overlooked that if the business fails the employees will also lose their means of making a living! Everybody plays a vital part, some smaller than others, but never less than necessary to smooth overall functioning.

The problem with nations that practice capitalism is that those at the top get to keep all surplus gain to divvy up at their own discretion. That's why slavery—exploitation without true wages or benefits—was so darned profitable for the slave owners. That's why minimum wage is kept at a minimum.

The great wealth that chief executive officers, owners and, producers are privileged to accumulate under such a system is all the incentive needed to maintain the status quo. Ours is a society in love with possessions. All of the diversifying and restructuring, mergers and leveraged buyouts, corporate raiding, bankruptcy, refinancing, and so on, amounts to a grand game of power ping-pong with capital assets that are never meant to leave the game table!

The happenstance of being born middle or lower class blocks entrance for most of us into this high-stakes game room. Be sure that those born, or invited, into a world of such manufactured privileges rarely ever lose them. Even if one does take a fall, the privileged status handed to them at birth or by favor acts as a safety net that usually halts sudden plummets due to portfolio volatility several stories above the basement!

But it is the wage-earning laborers who live down in that basement who shed the blood, sweat, and tears that fuel the capital ventures of big business. They bend their backs beneath a load of uncertainties concerning their families' week to week, check to check subsistence. These are the people who are consistently at risk of losing the most as a result of their employer's "free" enterprising . . . risk not just of their family's means of support, but also of their own health, limbs, and very lives. The mutilated remains of common laborers and their families are strewn across our nation's history for all to see.

POISON IN THE EYES

Sensuous objects and material stuff . . . luxurious convenience and the power of wealth . . . international fame and unlimited access to travel and spend—this is "the good life" as portrayed before the hungry eyes of our youth.

"I've got to see it to believe it," it is said. It follows from that common phrase that what a person sees is what a person believes.

The tender minds of children are most easily infiltrated by the advertisements of a materialistic society. Like poison, the expectation of accumulation builds within their young systems and increases the scope of its damage for as long as commercial advertisements continue to be ingested.

It's not just the great stuff the kids see that the Joneses have collected and strategically displayed on their lawns and driveways—it's also the envy they see in Mommy and Daddy's eyes. It's the wallet full of money and the expensive Corvette that Michael down the block is always flashing. But, most of all, it's the child's best friend, the babysitter . . . good buddy T.V. Good buddy T.V. is always teaching about hype and glitz and splashy new toys and the things you've just *GOT* to have and movies you've just *GOT* to see because they're so totally excellent. T.V. commands greater attention than schoolteachers—**always teaching that Life is Things and that Things are Life.**

As we watch T.V. shows and movies, we must momentarily suspend our senses to believe that fiction is fact and that fantasy is reality; that "Indians" are bad guys, good guys who are "bad" are "cool," that Africans are savages, that Snow White is beautiful, that Tarzan is Lord, Europe is the birthplace of civilization, and that Americans are specially blessed by God for being so doggone independent. Good buddy T.V. doesn't respond to questions—picture tubes simply can't answer questions. Just accept what you see; feed and believe; hunger for more; don't buck the system; speak only when spoken to; conform to the mold; relax and breathe deeply; everything's fine . . . virtual reality's almost here; learn to see things our way . . . our way . . . our way.

I offer the following provocative passage taken from a critique on this current state of affairs by Jerry Mander (1978) in his book "Four Arguments for the Elimination of Television":

> Seeing is believing. Like many an axiom, this one is literally true. Only since the ascendancy of the media has this been opened to question. Throughout . . . generations of human existence, whatever we saw with our eyes was concrete and reliable. Experience was directly between us and the natural environment. Non mediated. Non processed. Not altered by other humans. The question of what is real and unreal is itself a new one, abstract and impossible to understand. The natural . . . design is for humans to see all things as real, since the things we see have always been real. Seeing things on television as false and unreal is learned. It goes against nature . . . Western society, biased toward the objective mental mode of experience, tends to be blind not only to the power of images, but also to the fact that we are nearly defenseless against their effect. Since we are educated and thoughtful, as we like to think, we believe we can choose among the things that will influence us. We accept fact, we reject lies. We go to the movies, we watch television, we see photographs, and as their images pour into us, we believe we can choose among those we wish to absorb and those we don't. We assume that our rational processes will protect us from implantation, or brainwashing. What we fail to realize is the difference between fact and image. There is no rejection of images. Raise your eyes from the page a moment. Look about your room. Can you reject what you are seeing?
>
> (pp. 246,252,257,258)

The answer is no. What is seen is eaten—and we become what we eat. The preeminence of material stuff is what fuels the bellies of America. And in the midst of the feeding frenzy we further and further poison ourselves . . . and right now our children are being stuffed with sicker stuff than even we ever swallowed.

Fast-Food Syndrome

A brief commentary here on the reason for faster and faster food . . . **the drive to satisfy lusts instantaneously.** To consume as if it was this nation's mandate by God. To consume faster than what we consume can be paid for, or its supply can be regenerated. To attempt to consume in quantities so vast that what is consumed cannot possibly be digested—and what there is no room left for our stomachs to consume is thrown into the overflowing garbage pails, bins, and barges that are emptied to clog America's landfills and waterways. So much wasted material . . . and now we're running out of places to dispose of it. We're glutting our oceans with our treated sewage, overflowing our garbage dumps, constipating our biosphere.

Microwaveable *this*—ready in-an-instant and pre-prepared *that*—cooked in a flash if you just add water. Here's my money, where's my food. No struggle. No sweat. No need to think about the fact that while our faces are pleasantly stuffed with more food than our obese bodies really need or can make use of, that gentleman . . . see, that one right over there . . . digs down deep into that black bag of trash on the street corner to find just a remnant of a sandwich to chew on or a discarded can with a sip of warm soda.

"The Boasting Of What He Has And Does"

Not too long ago in the history of humankind, throughout the 17th–19th centuries, in a little area of the world called "Western Europe" during a period labeled the Enlightenment, men instituted a philosophy that would subvert all existing notions of Humanity's place in the world. The "Western European" male would be made the standard against which to define all other people; the "West" would be promoted as the hub around which all other societies must revolve; "Progress" became the measuring stick by which the practices and artifacts of all other cultures were evaluated for worth. To feel able to define other lives . . . to be willing to contain, control, or destroy those lives at whim . . . might lead anyone to get real high on themselves! America has merely inherited the Western legacy.

Let's be fair, though. This has all happened before. Self-centeredness and posing as the greatest thing that has ever come along—this has been the hallmark of every society ever graced with the label of "civilization" . . . every society that grew too big to sit still in its own britches. Egypt. Babylon. Assyria. Persia. Ethiopia. The Aztecs. Rome. Greece. Phoenicia. China. Portugal. Spain. Great Britain. France. Germany. Italy. Japan. The United States. There is no culture, past or present, that isn't guilty of the self-centered boast and of erecting monuments to its own greatness.

But self-promotion and propaganda also bring a harsh denial of the miseries we create and perpetuate. Lying to ourselves comes as the cost of a *pretense* of greatness. When we can walk briskly past the starving homeless or the hopeless child, we've learned to play the game very well. We only glimpse those discarded by our society as phantoms . . . images with no nerve endings . . . of no consequence to our daily lives. See no evil. Hear no evil. No speaking. No embracing. No acknowledgment.

DISENGAGEMENT.
DETACHMENT.
DISCONNECTION.

In America, apathy has become an art form. Consequently, leisurely concern and recreational aid campaigns have come into fashion. What pretends to be involvement is most often accompanied by the whispers of, "What am I gonna get out of this?" Or, "I'll feel so good for doing this." Or, "Sure, I'll donate a **little** of my time." We've forgotten how to come together just for the sake of each other's company. Someone whispers, "But shouldn't we all be responsible for taking care of ourselves??" Yeah, and that's why we're falling apart.

DYSFUNCTION.

We are a nation entrapped within the lethal devices of our own extravagant indulgences—the harvest for our self-centered inventions is finally being returned to us; the darkness in America is getting darker. New forms of mental illness and psychological disorders. New diseases that disrupt and destroy the functions of the human body. Something is dreadfully wrong . . . and worsening.

Why then do we announce ourselves as the masters of our own destinies? Why do we claim we're enjoying the freedoms of our inalienable rights? Why do we take so much credit for the spread of "peace and prosperity" throughout the world? The huge problems that loom in front of our nation have been ballooning out of control for years. We regularly complain of too much crime, too much fear, too much politics, too much greed, too much stress, too much frustration, too much uncertainty, too much unrest, too much unfairness, too much consumption, and too much hate infesting the communities we live in. Whatever we Americans have been spreading abroad over recent decades, the state of the world we live in now is hardly what anyone would dare call healthy!

What more is there to say about the failing state of our nation that isn't visible on the nightly telecasts of your local and network news? And every night we also see that the conditions in any other nation you can name are just as bad or much, much worse! So what's the answer?

Every problem has an answer, *if only we can comprehend it, and then have the courage to apply it!* **It is evident that our hope must lie in a power that can overcome the gravity of our human condition!** The question is: Is this repair possible by human hands, or must our salvation at this desperate stage be given over to hands capable of far more strength than the whole of Humanity owns or has ever thought possible?

STOP AND THINK.

The country I live in,
my place on the globe,
has made certain failings
accessible to me.
Now that these failings are a part of my family and culture
have I allowed them to break down
the integrity of my living?

LIVE A LIFE WORTH GIVING.

CRYING IN THE DARK

The nearness of answers
remains yet elusive;

the song of significance
mocks me
abuses my sense of hope
with hopeless conclusions
beating back the enthusiasm my spirit once flowed
as it eagerly sought to reason and question,
to know and to prove,
to be sure,
to be certain;
to stand strong in my stubborn beliefs.

But, alas, it never worked for me.

For all the strain . . . the grasping . . . the reaching . . .
my hand always got slapped away by my weakness
before I could touch my relief;
before my efforts
manufactured my peace . . .

and still I do not know.

I just don't know.

There's so much I don't know if I'll ever know;
so much that might fill my paths with light
and help my darkened eyes with sight
and grant new life to one like me.

oh God, I need . . .
reveal to me

help for my hopeful plea
won't You please?

what I'm doing now
just isn't working.

Chapter 3

In Search Of A Balanced Point Of View

"... but I still haven't found what I'm looking for ..."

(line from a popular song by the rock band "U2")

On sunny afternoons after school, all the kids came outside to play. The air would fill with echoes going back and forth between the red brick and stone buildings on both sides of our narrow street. Pounding rubber balls, the taps and scratches of shoe heels, and the slapping of sneakers on the cement and asphalt.

Sometimes white chalk would appear, and hopscotch boxes were quickly drawn on the neat squares of cement pavement in front of my Grandma's house. Grandma lived next door to us. Houses on our block were side by side, sharing each other's walls.

On a particular day, similar to other days, I watched as a small flat stone was tossed to bounce across the cement into a numbered box. I watched the one foot, two feet, one foot hops from box to box to stop and balance on one small hopping foot, steadying itself, to drop a hand to pick up the stone. Some little girl came to sit beside me and asked me to look at her. We were sitting on one of Grandma's two wooden benches, just inside the front gate. Two steps down was the sidewalk and other kids. I ignored the girl. I made sure my body had no contact with hers on the bench. Why was she talking to me anyway? Didn't she see I didn't have anything I wanted to say?

"Look at me!" she said, tugging at my arm.

"Will you stop it!" I snapped back, jerking my arm away. Being touched was not natural to me. My family didn't touch me. I tightened the skin of my eyebrows and the bridge of my nose into a frown.

"Smile!" the little girl said slyly, trying to tickle me.

"Leave me alone!" I yelled. I tried to move away from the touching. I must have grinned. Grinning relaxes the frowns on faces.

The girl clapped a hand over her mouth, all giggles.

I asked what she was laughing so loud for.

The kids out in front of us now had our attention. I felt like I was now being watched. I can't remember the faces, just the noise and voices that seemed to stop. The little girl stood up, pointed at my face and declared, finger in my face, pointing, speaking out loud, "Look! He only has *one* dimple! See?! Look at his face!"

"No I don't," I said, dropping my face, my eyes, my voice. My head was down and I didn't want to see if anyone was looking. The attention made my face warm and I needed to move away fast.

"No I don't," I repeated, stiffly. My whole head seemed to glow brightly, very hot, drawing lots of attention. I was beneath windows, very near, on both sides of the street, always with onlookers. I rushed through the painted iron gate, going quickly next door, upstairs to "our house," to the second floor apartment we lived in, down the hallway so dark after the bright outside, around a curve and a corner, into the bathroom, closing the door behind me.

Locking the door, I didn't have to turn on the light to see. There was a light well in the center of the house, right beside the bathroom. I waited patiently for my eyes to adjust to the murky sun working its way through the frosted glass in the small window above and to the right of the toilet. I wanted the dimness. I wanted the coolness. I wanted the silence. I wanted the tile walls to feel close to me.

I sat on the edge of the sink. It was clean white porcelain. I had shorts on, but the surface warmed quickly against my bare legs as they made contact. In front of the bathroom medicine cabinet mirror, above the sink, I stared long at my face. The house was quiet. Everyone else was outside.

Everyone else knew that you either have two dimples or no dimples at all. You could see that from all the illustrations and photographs and pictures in books and magazines. I was certain. But in the soft, chubby skin of my left cheek was the only dimple I could manage. Although I strained or poked at my tiring, smiling face muscles, my right cheek remained undented. I poked and I strained. I poked and I strained. I made my face muscles move every way I could think of. I stared at my face.

That was when I decided I would never let anyone else notice there was something very wrong with me. As much as I could help it, as much as I could keep anyone else from knowing my secret, I would never let anyone else see my smile.

I was asked to smile for this school photograph . . . I am straining not to do so. My entire body is straining to <u>not</u> do as I was told, even while doing as I was told.

How do we become so certain of ourselves? Our strengths? Our faults? Can anyone really state with certainty that their own perception of themselves is clear and unimpeded? Looking in a mirror, it's been said that "the hardest thing to see is me"—and it is usually because our character flaws are in the way!

In order to correct what appear to us as the imbalances in our lives, we are often willing to attempt the most extreme and painful contortions. Yet after the best of our most religiously perfunctory efforts, the potential of our lives can remain an atrophied, unstretched thing. I know this was true of myself. Even though I first made the decision to withhold my smile while I was still a child, I didn't suddenly become wiser as I grew up. I had no reason to think that my reasoning was flawed. I was as intelligent as anyone else. What could I have gained from what anyone else might have had to say about the ugliness of having only one dimple? Only God knows, because among men I kept my painful self-image private.

Perhaps it is impossible, on our own, to see the "big picture" regarding what ails us and what would best aid us. Perhaps that's why we go to doctors and specialists and trusted friends for the outsider's point of view we need to help us pinpoint the problem. Our sense of imbalance naturally alerts us that we're in need of some kind of help . . . but our sense of imbalance also leaves us disoriented, weakened, and inhibits our attempts to correct the problem.

The more off balance we are, the more difficult it is to see what we should be looking for. One thing is for sure—if there's something wrong with us, we'll need the help of someone who can see the overall picture—someone through whom we might just catch an inspiring glimpse of the big map for our lives.

SEVERED TIES

At a glance, it is evident that human beings share a social instinct. We seek out opportunities to belong to groups—gangs or lodges, clubs or organizations—that allow their members a sense of importance, responsibility, and cooperation. These are the things true families are made of. There's a raw power to this impulse to band together and to pool the resources of all who belong, increasing the collective strength of the group. This is the impulse that generates the strength of parental and family ties, ensuring our survival from the time we are born. This is the impulse that generates the strength of our communities, multiplying and reinforcing their numbers and prospering them over generations.

The fact that this behavior is common to all also means that it isn't an accident of nature. It has somehow been built into us. It's how human needs are met. Our willingness to cooperate with the strengths that others bring to bear along with our own will always prove the surest method of accomplishing any of life's demands!

Yet, while many of us were still in diapers, those who raised us encouraged us to believe that the world must revolve around *me, the baby*. It's a wonder that babies don't raise a whole lot more ruckus when the time comes to teach them they can only get their way *sometimes*! Our personal "declarations of independence" interfere with the great lesson that needs to be taught to all children: *that to live for self, taking care of what's best for me first, reduces the time I spend helping and connecting; reduces my importance to the everyday lives of the "family" members who share their lives with me; reduces my reason for being here at all*. What a shame to be given all that makes me unique in the universe and then waste it all serving myself!

Consider this, please. If I were to help a member of my very own "family" to pull his or her life together at a moment when, because of a needful condition, he or she happens to be weaker than I, it doesn't require much effort to think how much my whole extended "family" and I stand to gain. When one of our members begins to grow in the stature of his or her living, the whole "family" is strengthened! A strong and extending family can always provide within itself resources that must otherwise somehow be found or purchased.

This question follows: If bonding into "family" groupings is our inborn inclination, and our natural desire is to feel like we "belong" to a group and borrow freely from the strength they offer us—what is it that makes us so **ridiculously** stingy with our personal resources? Instead of sharing ourselves with the "family of Humanity," why are we sabotaging our living?

It seems we have lost our linkage to an important truth here. TRUTH, by definition, possesses an enduring quality, reliable, *never* changing, and *never* passing away. Meanwhile, what we have are enormous numbers of our fellow humanity wasting away in anguish. Some waste others away. "Waste 'em!!," is what the killers shout as they blow away their victims in today's action movie adventures. Others, we know, waste themselves, pulling the trigger over and over again, unable to keep from harming themselves. And *all* of us waste time and resources and some of the best we could offer to each other. But this is FALSE human living. **That which is FALSE is weak, undependable and is *always* lived in vain.** Wasted living eventually sputters out. **ONLY LIES DIE.**

We daily survey the mounting tragedy—the best of our lives is slipping away. All that might have been . . . the lost chances . . . the wasted potential . . . the missed opportunities . . . if only we lived truer lives. Before our eyes, our children are being devastated by the corruption that surrounds them. Sons and daughters are forced into traumatic sexual activity by family "friends" or relatives. Too many children are brought up to feel O.K. about giving birth to babies before they've finished being children. Too many sons are neglected by their fathers and left to learn win/lose strategies for their lives, that its okay to "do what you wanna do" . . . and that its best to "get the other guy before he gets you." Where do they learn this behavior? Kids will grow up to be what they consistently see. And if the culture predominately displays wasted and selfish living and dead ends, then our children will emulate what they see. They contain the next generation of terrorists and serial killers, racists and child molesters, perverts and addicts, and those paralyzed by their fears. Born to die, as they say.

But you may be one of those who want to live a life that isn't in vain and destined to fail. You may be one of those who have been searching to find your way home to that long-lost original place where human potential first sprung up and a life could be true and meaningful. You might also, then, have become aware that human potential tends to rot from the inside out. And so we begin our quest within because of yet another faint awareness: **THAT WHICH IS TRUE CANNOT BE QUENCHED. EVEN IN THE MIDST OF OUTER DEVASTATION, TRUTH *ALWAYS* RESURRECTS ITSELF.** So we endeavor to search for our true beginnings—the life-giving system, shared strength from which we've been torn.

Our search is for lost connections which are difficult to see—the withered state of the human condition—the cataclysmic starvations and genocides that occur somewhere in the world yearly shows we've been cut off for a while now. Our instinct is to try and save ourselves from withering away as well. It seems to us we've no alternative but to try and save ourselves. And we do try. When we've decided we have found a source that would make our living True again, our instinct for self-preservation kicks in. Like the lone leaf on a diseased and withering vine that is imminently threatened by the surrounding scourge, in desperation we detach ourselves in a last act of self-preservation. Yet, detached, we, like the leaf can only spiral downward.

Although we will not die today—although we will not strangle like the others trapped in the consuming blight—we will die just the same. It matters not how spiritual our detachment is, how monastic, and self-denying—detachment from the originating vine eventually leads to the same result. Even if we were barely subsisting before, there is little else that can feed us now except for the limited resources of whatever group we may have chosen to join. **How *do* we save ourselves??**

TORCHES IN THE DARKNESS

We are responsible for the consequences of our choices. We have chosen to live imbalanced lives, more self-centered than mutually supportive. A life centered in self is doomed to wither and perish, while a life centered in others can only grow in strength and foundation. The self-centered life's imbalances will cause it to fail. It wobbles and tips and topples and flutters away and is no longer here tomorrow. It is weak and untrue to the human design for mutual support.

Some people have entirely lost the awareness that we were meant to live abundantly, bearing fruit for many others to enjoy.

Some people live dazed by a million entertainments . . . or a million agonies . . . that render them far too distracted and dysfunctional to consider searching for home.

Some people are so caught in the grooves of self-destructive habits and intolerance for others that they couldn't pull up out the ditch now even if they wanted to. Most don't want to.

But some do make approaches to reacquire the missing element in their lives. Theirs is a movement to raise themselves upright by their own two hands; to balance themselves onto platforms made of statements of belief or catechisms, codes of conduct or morality, rituals and organized ceremonies—all constructed according to a human design to reconnect with the truth they know to be near. The goal for the searcher is to climb that platform, to rise above low-level living. To save themselves. To extend their lives beyond what exists right now. These hand-wrought platforms that true searchers struggle to climb are the constructions we call "**religion**."

Some religions stretch upward to reconnect us again to the one or many deities their searchers have concluded to be the infinite power that first made and can also recreate them.

Some religions stretch inward, because those searchers conclude that they alone hold the infinite power to make and recreate themselves.

Some religions stretch across from person to person, because those searchers have concluded that either in certain other human beings, or in the politics of society itself, lies that infinite power to revolutionize their lives and recreate world community.

We build our religions to carry us to the place where we may be saved. But how does this make common sense? We are not "gods" in ourselves—our neediness, our frailty, our failures, and our fast-approaching deaths eliminate that as a possibility. We are mere mortals. Can *anything* constructed by the limited reach of finite hands hope to bridge the infinite divide between the *falsehoods* of our lifestyles and the *truth* of our potential? Is it reasonable for us to strain to attain the highest sense of self—**isn't that the same old direction our self-centeredness has**

taken us all along? This self-absorbed bent, as we might imagine, makes religions rather easy to identify.

The lie of self-importance will be a mark of religion. Religions claim to enable us to build bridges to perfect wholeness, but all we have to build with are the motives of our *imperfect* hearts and minds! Anyone who attempts to construct a different bridge is spurned and disregarded in a fit of "holier-than-thou" indignation.

The lie of self-reliance will be a mark of religion. Religions have produced an independence and mutual disdain that has created barriers, factions, sects, and denominations amongst groups that ironically teach of the "family" of humankind or the necessity of brotherhood. Instead of family, though, there's feuding. Instead of community, there's conflict and quarreling.

And the lie of self-indulgence will be a mark of religion. Religious practices make it incredibly easy to justify behavioral extremes—from rituals of rigid exactitude, to conspicuous demonstrations of self-deprivation, to pretentious displays of self-absorbed dedication—all based on a belief of having attained an elevated mindset among men and women and intended to reinforce a self-promoting and often political agenda.

All the effort that goes into maintaining a high "moral" or fully "realized" outlook defies common sense. It's time to for us to come back to earth. It is from that humble position that some of us have come to realize an easier way home: instead of hopelessly grasping for that which is infinitely beyond our reach, we choose to ask for help from someone with the appropriate arm length. That's why little children come to adults for help. Isn't it time we adults get as wise as our children and confess that, like them, our arms aren't long enough to reach what we need? If we admit that the things we construct have the terrifying tendency to collapse into ruins, then we may come to realize the answer to that famously religious question, "How can I find God?"

The answer: YOU COULD SPEND YOUR WHOLE LIFE REACHING, BUT YOU'LL NEVER MANAGE TO STRETCH ACROSS THE CHASM THAT DIVIDES YOUR IMPERFECT CONDITION FROM GOD'S UNLIMITED PERFECTION.

Perhaps, for starters, we can admit our need for help from an arm greater than our own. Help which is able to bridge the canyon dividing the important living we seek from our current limitations. But what medium exists that could bridge such glorious living to our frailty . . . and keep us from being engulfed in the chasm that lies between?

THE NATURE OF THE CASE

Facing any sort of medical emergency, you would first seek to familiarize yourself with the procedure your physician has decided will heal your particular ailment.

As we have seen, a severe dysfunction now besets the body of Humanity, with tendencies passed along from parent to child, from century to century. No generation has ever been free from these symptoms: *pride and the lust for power to fuel that pride; degenerate and abusive sexual practices; vice, atrocity, and the invention of new kinds of evil; the idolatrous placement of the self, nature, human ideologies, or material objects as "sacred" fixtures so as to receive the worship, adoration, and reverence of our hearts; the self-predictive practices of astrology, the occult, witchcraft, or the dark spiritual pursuits; disunity and independent living; self-serving ambition; fearful hatred; fits of rage; unreasonable jealousy; murderous hostility, strife, and the splintering apart into opposing groups and contentious factions; unquenchable greed and malicious envy; the drunken abandonment of wisdom or sensibility to indulge in unthinking orgies of self-appeasement.*

That is the diagnosis. Humanity is in a grave condition. The longer things remain in such a state, the faster death grabs its next victim.

We humans are full of spirit; it is our spirits that animate these piles of flesh. But we humans have seen our collective spirit become a stagnant swamp—congested with layer upon layer of the sediment of many deteriorating lives. Nearby, the Fountain of human life, the Supply that first birthed us is still superabounding with new Life. But we're out of touch with the easy remedy for our ills. **The simplest remedy for clearing a stopped-up system is to inject an agent that will flush out the blockages, blow out the sediment, and carry in a rush of reviving refreshment!**

But, it must be emphasized that such a remedy can only be initiated from the outside in! **That which has become corrupted cannot, of its own corrupted resources, reverse the process of deterioration. Rather, a cleansing or healing agency, untainted by that corruption, must be INTRODUCED into that failing condition.** All a stagnant body of water can do on its own is continue to stand still and stink! It can do absolutely nothing to cleanse itself—IT *CAN* HOWEVER SUBMIT TO THE INRUSH OF A SAVING FLOW OF FRESH RUNNING WATER. Only therein will come renewal.

Such an operation would have to extend its reach into our innermost depths; it is our polluted spirits that most need to be touched by the help of a fresh introduction. Our imbalanced lives could finally find their equilibrium. A *great* change in humanity's faltering course *can* take place.

STOP AND THINK.

For as long as has been recorded
the efforts of the human race
have consistently risen,
and then fallen.
There is no other precedent.
Life is brief.
It is in my best interest
to take my one stand
not on a platform built by flesh and blood hands,
a platform which warps from year to year,
a shifting foundation made of wood and clay
but rather
to find footing on the mountaintop
that is made of solid rock
and won't give way beneath me.

LIVE A LIFE WORTH GIVING.

my GOD?

although i am cut off from
You
and weak

too weak to reach
You

my God
hear my whisper.

i've heard You really love me . . .
even though . . .
well . . .

You see the way i am.

i finally know my need.
but . . .
well . . .

i cannot find You.

my God
You
are infinity

i'm lost
You see

can You find me please?

Chapter 4

An Extraordinarily Special Offer

"Like water spilled on the ground, which cannot be recovered, so we must die. But God does not take away life; instead, he devises ways so that a banished person may not remain estranged from him."

The Bible (2 Samuel 14:14)

"You lied, Ma," I repeated, digging in for a display of remorse. My mother—her eyes dutifully upon the road ahead—at this point merely hissed at me, her anger seeping through the back of the skull silhouetted directly in front of me. Oh yes, I was burning too. We were on our way home from "The Wiz," the all-black remake of "The Wizard of Oz," starring Diana Ross, Michael Jackson, Nipsey Russell and a big brown man in a lion costume easin' on down a dirty yellow brick road. The audience seemed to enjoy it all right up to the end, but I hadn't really seen it. Only that lie before the lights went out, that lie while the soundtrack grooved, that lie as I was being yanked with the rest of the kids into the night that'd befallen Brooklyn outside the discount theater.

Chris, Angie and Mark were a heap of arms and torsos fallen in upon each other on the opposite side of the rear seat, mouths suckling breath. I slid my cheek against the glass on my side of the car. Outside was movement and mind play, cause and effect. But all I knew for certain was a brand new adolescent sense of violation, the coolness of glass, and the inertia carrying our banana-yellow 1973 Pontiac back to a man who would love it long after its skin had begun to rot.

My father kept it parked in front of our building where the rest of us watched it overtaken with rust until it was easier for him to pay 40-something dollars a month to keep it in the lot further down Lincoln Place owned by the Puerto Rican lady. The engine stopped cooperating and he couldn't move the car out of the way of the street sweepers jetting fluids, brushing the gutters clean. That banana Pontiac sat browning in the sun in that lot for another couple of years before he finally let go. He was real stubborn that way . . . doing what he wanted, rather than what was needed. What we needed. After thirty years of marriage, my mother got tired of the struggle to find reasons to stay.

I did not believe I was like my father at all except for sharing the same first name, middle name, and last name on my birth certificate. He once concluded I keep a beard so as not to look like him and that I studied architecture so as not to be an artist like him and that he knew me better than I know myself. So he said. I swear I wasn't like him. Recently he had been saying he's proud of me. I'm not proud of what he did to the family.

Back home, I sat down at the sturdy little desk in the bedroom Chris and I shared. I don't know what they did with the other kids, but the only traces of life in the apartment at that time of night were my heartbeat and the whispering outside the door just before my father appeared at the far end of the room.

I was almost twelve years old; I'd be starting high school next year. I'd never before heard of a mother lying. Angie and Mark were both *over* 6 years old, and Ma passed them through as 6 or younger so she could purchase their tickets at the discount. And that she would do so on *purpose* . . . well, that was my defense anyway. Shading me from the glare of the single 60-watt ceiling bulb, my father asked me if Ma had actually *spoken* a lie to anyone about anything at all. An unforeseen exercise in logic this was, and I was surprised that I could do nothing but acknowledge that my mother uttered barely a word beyond the customary "Thank you" as she requested her tickets.

I had nothing to hold on to, imperceptibly pressing myself backwards into the crevices of the furniture. No more words. He reaches forward and removes the glasses from my face; I follow his hands with my eyes as he lays them aside on the desk. Handicapped, I squint as the blur of his right hand disappears into a clapping thudding against the left side of my face. Inertia takes me on another ride as my weight pitches, muscles firing, the legs of the chair shifting opposite the blow, my inner ear numbs and, a new blindness sparkling, chair and I go twisting on one wooden leg, tilting, unable to escape the gravity of the moment, bouncing heavily once and then again against the dull linoleum floor.

I can generate little more than some errant, uncoordinated attempts to rise. I need to get up. Wood rattling, I inch along a taut moment of time failing in my effort to detach myself from chair. I'm expected to get myself up. The outside corner of my left eye flickers violently and will do so from time to time for years thereafter. In the distance, Ma's voice muffles Doppler-like toward me from the doorway at the opposite corner of the room; I can make out her soft shape rushing in and out of my sightline between my father's pants legs. It is she who gathers me with maternal economy from the cool floor against my ripening cheek.

I allowed her to hold on.

Not long after, I acquired the vocabulary word *deceived,* increasing my ability to express what I meant, another link in my armor against my father's final judgements.

I told this story as an example of how badly things can go wrong if one cannot properly express a besetting problem. The first three chapters of this book have constituted a sort of damage assessment of the common human being and, consequently, of human society. We've observed that if we're looking for the world around us to carry us to safety we're all in trouble, because our support system isn't quite sound. To know that something is <u>wrong</u> with the way things are now, is to acknowledge a *right* that should be present, but isn't! A sense of this rightness can be revealed to some degree by this equation:

What is <u>PART TRUE OR UNTRUE = ALL LIE OR UNRELIABLE</u>;

Unless something stands eternally established and unchangeable it cannot be considered Truth. **IF SOMETHING DOESN'T STAND UNCHANGING, THEN THAT THING WILL EVENTUALLY DESCEND INTO A FORM OF FALSEHOOD, ITS MEANING DISSOLVING AND RESHAPING ITSELF OVER THE COURSE OF TIME.** Accordingly, if you find the opposite to a falsehood, you've discovered a truth. We've already made a record of falsehoods to work from—be prepared to let them go in order to receive an injection of truth.

PERSONAL DAMAGE

Self-importance is a falsehood, a lie. Placing one's "self" on a pedestal is meaningless. Anyone absorbed with being lifted up in the eyes of others will be up there on that pedestal all alone, with no room to draw shoulder to shoulder with anyone else. And even if there was any room, it's impossible to help brace up another's life when self-centeredness disconnects the ties that would otherwise bind us together. The truth is, authentic human living must practice a **co-operation**, where the only claim to importance is in being a fruit-bearing, supportive branch of humanity's "family tree."

Self-reliance is another lie. Only the dead have neither the responsibility of dependents nor the need to depend. If you are alive, then even before birth the course of your life was already guided by its dependencies—a dependency on a life-supporting umbilical cord, a dependency on a relationship with a mother compelled to respond specifically to your needs. The truth is, authentic human living must practice an **interdependency**, wherein the resources for personal growing and strengthening are so freely given and received that every individual's life and sustenance is maximized.

Self-indulgence is a lie. It is not true to those who indulge themselves. Attempting to satisfy oneself in the extreme does not result in satisfaction, but an even more insatiable need that eventually demands greater indulgences! Only one thing universally satisfies, young or old, rich or poor: receiving and/or giving unconditional love. The truth is, authentic human living must practice an **all-embracing love** shared according to the need of those within one's sphere of living who lack love.

The purpose of the exercise we've just completed is this: **we must possess a working knowledge of how a system must *ideally* function in order to identify the best point of entry through which to introduce the remedy for its *malfunctioning*.** Comparing the LIE of what exists now with the TRUTH of the ideal that therefore must be, these things become starkly clear:

1) INDIVIDUALS ARE SOLELY RESPONSIBLE FOR THE DAMAGE WE HAVE DONE TO OURSELVES.

2) IT IS UPON MY OWN PERSON THAT DAMAGE I HAVE DONE HAS HAD ITS MOST DEVASTATING EFFECT.

3) THE RESULT OF THE DAMAGE IS THAT I FAIL TO CARRY OUT MY AUTHENTIC ROLE OF STRENGTHENING THE LIVES OF ALL THOSE I'M IN TOUCH WITH.

These conclusions arise from the following facts:

1) IT IS, FIRST, THE INDIVIDUAL WHO STEPS FORWARD FROM SOCIETY TO PROCLAIM THE MANY FALSEHOODS OF SELF-CENTERED "LIVING."

2) IT IS THE SAME INDIVIDUAL WHO EVENTUALLY TAILSPINS AND CRASHES INTO THE UNIQUE PERSONAL CONSEQUENCES OF SELF-CENTERED "LIVING."

3) INDIVIDUALS MAKE THEIR OWN UNIQUE CHOICES TO FACILITATE THEIR SPIRAL DOWNWARD FROM THE HEIGHTS OF POTENTIAL THEY CAN NEVER ATTAIN TO.

This is all to say that our damage is strictly personal.

A Parable of Rescue

Picture this story in your mind. You are on a walk in the cool shade of a sunlit garden with your Family. You are incredibly alive—there are so many things to think of, to do, and to create, and all eternity ahead of you! As a matter of fact, circumstances are so bright you're actually aglow. You could continue traveling along with the Family, with Father leading the way . . . but a thought occurs to you.

"I could lead the way!"

The thought appeals to something within you. You decide you can prove this. So in plain sight you publicly rebel against your Father's leadership and stomp off loudly in a direction of your own choosing. And you notice that the further you go from the Family, the dimmer the sun seems to shine. In spite of this, you stop at a fruit tree and begin tearing at its branches, just to prove to yourself you can do as you please!

You glance over your shoulder just to make sure your Family can see how independent you are. "People had better learn to look up to me!" you snort. "I'm very important!" you yell up to the heavens. Then the thought occurs, you can *make* everyone look up to you.

You look down at the crushed berries at your feet, seeping into the earth. An idea occurs. "I will dig a pit and hide it so that when someone comes in my direction, they will fall in and be trapped and have to look up to me. Then I will be the one on top of things. So you get down on your hands and knees and begin to dig . . . furiously, forcefully, mindlessly. You dig and dig until you yourself are totally hidden within the pit.

You finally feel that the pit is deep enough—but abruptly all the dirt you've been placing your weight on shifts and gives way. You lose your balance, grasp the air, face the sky, then the earth, then the sky again as you slide and topple noisily down a slimy embankment. Your body slaps hard against a pool of thick cold quagmire; you are partially swallowed beneath its loathsome surface. Mounds of loose dirt come down on your head. The light is gone—and you know, with sudden dread, that you no longer even glow.

The darkness down here is swallowing light just as quickly as it swallowed you. Reacting in terror, your hands stab upward and claw into the slime that was your pathway down. You jerk your body up against the pull of this miry weight with every fiber of your strength— only causing you to sink deeper into the bog!

With each passing moment of your immersion in this clinging befoulment, an uneasy irritation starts to blanket over your skin . . . and begins . . . yes, it begins to burn! You smell a rotten odor rising—as from an animal long dead in the sun. Then, as your skin begins to crawl and you lift your dripping fingers to scratch the itch consuming your face, the sharp stench that suddenly pierces your nostrils says it's your *own* flesh you smell in decay!

And then you feel the sickness beginning its creep, all chilly and cold, turning your stomach, pushing toward the center of your shivering body from every place in contact with the repulsive sludge. You know you're contaminated. Decomposing. Dying. You have been invaded by a malignancy. Like a cancer. Only you sense . . . no, you **know** . . . this is different. This is much different. This is worse than uncleanness. This is worse than illness. And this is a deadly and contagious disease.

Strength drains quickly as you continue to sink. You sense that what is happening to you, you are not able to halt. If you survived now, the rest of your days wouldn't be pleasant anyway. Suddenly, you are appalled to realize there is someone else right beside you!! Whoever it is, the terror in their eyes reveal a struggle as desperate as your own. And as your eyes continue to adjust to the darkness, you realize that you cannot even count the numbers of other failing bodies facing their doom down here with you. You join your voice with some of those who are crying to each other for help, but you quickly realize that no one in this pit is in any position or strong enough condition to lift anyone else back up to the warmth of the garden.

It is then that you notice that many are no longer even struggling. They float exhausted on their backs in the filth and seem to have grown quite accustomed to the conditions! They float slowly in and out of the shadows until a current takes over and begins to pull them quickly toward the massive black structure that towers erect in the distance. The closer the many other captives are drawn into this central darkness, they explode into an awful thrashing, and then completely disappear beneath the surface.

You hear a base and fitful laughter which you are certain comes from that equally massive figure sitting obscured at the heart of that structure, which sits raised up like . . . a throne! With this awakening understanding of your fate, you attempt to save yourself again, even though you're more exhausted than ever by the nausea and the struggle to stay afloat. With your energies being rapidly consumed, you decide your only hope is to try to work your way up to the sun where you know you really belong. If you work hard enough, you believe you can find your way out of the mire . . . controlled breathing exercises . . . positive thinking . . . summoning together all your remaining energies . . . a systematic expenditure of your very own effort designed to elevate you upwards to salvation. *A RELIGION.*

You try. But the truth of physics never changes. *The only way to possibly counteract a force that is pulling in one direction is with at least an equal force pulling in the opposite direction.* Nothing you do will save you unless you can generate the self-effort to overmatch the force that draws you under. And, frankly, at this point your arms are too weak, the weight of your body too heavy to even keep from slipping beneath the sludge. **There's only one place that your help is going to come from . . . only one place where enough strength and leverage can be generated to lift you out in opposition to the downward tug dragging you to oblivion.** *Look upward, because your help is going to come from above! Someone from above is going to have to find you and take it upon himself to exert the strength necessary to pull you up from the sucking morass.*

A Source of Truth

What does the preceding parable suggest to us? Of course, it's just a parable. I made it up as a way of representing a particular view of the human condition. You may disagree with its accuracy . . . but I didn't write it for accuracy. You may be disturbed by its bleak view of the human spirit . . . but I didn't write it to make you feel cozy.

You may want to close the book at this point and hide it up high on a shelf, but before you do so, ask yourself this question: Do any of the words you've read thus far reflect a portion of your reality? Can you recognize yourself in it? A loved one? Does it ring true? Is it plausible?

However you respond, know this—this parable has been my testimony. This has been my life. The parable I have laid out is a representation of how lost I really was. What about yourself? Are you lost? Do you need someone to find you and lift you up out of the sucking clay?

Three messages are laid out in the preceding parable—let's look carefully at them:

1) My efforts to lift myself to my own salvation are futile!

2) All my help will arrive from above—there is **nothing** I can do but call for it and wait for that help to reach down to meet me where I am, at the level of my need!

3) Someone in particular is going to need to personally intercede into my desperate situation and labor to lift me higher!

THERE IS ONLY ONE DOCUMENT ESTEEMED UNIVERSALLY BY ALL RELIGIONS THAT DIRECTLY CORROBORATES ALL THE ABOVE. THIS DOCUMENT IS THE BEST-SELLING BOOK IN THE WORLD—THE COLLECTION OF BOOKS CALLED *THE BIBLE*!

THE ONLY TESTAMENT OF PERSONAL INTERVENTION ON OUR BEHALF

It is obvious now that the damage to humanity is based on the personal dysfunction of the billions of individuals that constitute it as a whole; **the damage is to our individual and uniquely fashioned persons!** So where do we go from here? As concluded at the end of the previous chapter, we know that it is inconceivable for a body, once fallen into impurity and cut off from its original source of fresh supply, to at the same time harbor its own cleansing flow! Once the process that leads to putrefaction has begun, and healthy bodily functions have diminished, there's no escaping the inevitable end **unless somehow you are *rescued*!** In accord with these three criteria drawn from my testimony and preceding parable, it is written:

1) **"What a wretched man I am! Who will rescue me from this body of death?"**

(Romans 7: 24)

"For it is by grace you have been saved, through faith—and this not from yourselves, it is the gift of God—not by works, so that no one can boast."

(Ephesians 2: 8, 9)

2) **"I lift up my eyes to the hills—where does my help come from? My help comes from the LORD, the Maker of heaven and earth."**

(Psalm 121: 1, 2)

"I waited patiently for the LORD; he turned to me and heard my cry. He lifted me out of the slimy pit, out of the mud and mire; he set my feet on a rock and gave me a firm place to stand."

(Psalm 40: 1, 2)

3) **"Come and see what God has done, how awesome his works in man's behalf!"**

(Psalm 66: 5)

"For I have come down from heaven not to do my will but to do the will of him who sent me. And this is the will of him who sent me, that I shall lose none of all that he has given me, but raise them up [to new life] at the last day."

(John 6: 38, 39)

In direct accord with the criteria for salvation as drawn from the earlier parable, stands the Bible. In my life, in my situation, it rings true. This is a spiritual document quoted across the boundaries of the major world faiths, and held in esteem for its sacredness throughout history. It would appear to be to our benefit to continue searching the Bible for more truths we might gather about our fatal living and the prescription for our cure. We will undoubtedly find many more of these truths—a tree that bears a specific fruit will always continue to bear that fruit and only that type of fruit. In fact, the type of fruit identifies the essential nature of its tree! Let's taste some more of this fruit and see what TRUTH the Bible is really made of.

SIN = A CONTAMINANT CONTRACTED AS A CONSEQUENCE OF UNTRUE LIVING

I present to you this startling summation of our human Nature: **Truth is immortal. Yet, every human being who is born soon dies. If that which is true always endures, then every mortal human being is somehow born as a hollow misrepresentation of that which they are called to be. Our living becomes as futile, unstable, and inconsistent as a lie. Thus, we die. If we were true—if we were what we ought to be—each of us would endure and never pass away.** In other words, since everyone dies, we must all be hollow, contradictory versions of what we ought to be. Our light goes out—as it did within "you" trapped within the pit in the parable. The Bible provides a source of Truth that once again illumines our insight:

> "Behold, [the wicked man] conceives iniquity and is pregnant with mischief and gives birth to lies. He has made a pit and hollowed it out and has fallen into the hole which he made [before the trap was completed]. His mischief shall fall back in return upon his own head, and his violence come down [with loose dirt] upon his own scalp."
> (Psalm 7:14–16; The Amplified Bible)

> "For God cannot be tempted by evil, nor does he tempt anyone; but each one is tempted when, by his own evil desire, he is dragged away and enticed. Then, after desire has conceived, it gives birth to sin; and sin, when it is full-grown, gives birth to death."
> (James 1:13–15)

It is absolutely vital to note that God has nothing to do with a person's fall into the "pit." **It is a matter of INDIVIDUAL choice and it has**

consequences that are INHERITED. The Bible calls that entrapping pit *sin*. An independent course of living by self-determined choices always winds up with that frightening fatal plummet into the pit of darkness. Death. How can we best understand this *sin* the Bible speaks of?? The Bible has already communicated one definition with such direct simplicity that I can only build upon it:

> "Anyone, then, who knows the good he ought to do and doesn't do it, sins."
>
> (James 4:17)

First, there is the personal choice to stand in opposition to the proven goodness of God the Creator. The desire here is to be considered foremost . . . to be honored as being important in oneself . . . to be prized and applauded . . . to be followed and obeyed . . . to be the center of events . . . to be taken care of first. **The evil in this desire is to choose to live the lie of SELF-IMPORTANT PRIDE.** This is sin.

Second, there is the personal choice to hold in contempt the wisdom of unity, the source of strength conceived from the mind of God Almighty. The desire here is to stand stubbornly apart with only the pretense of an assumed authority as the ill-equipped nucleus of one's own strength, control, and impulse. **The evil in this desire is to choose to live the lie of SELF-RELIANT INDEPENDENCE.** This too is sin.

Third, there is the personal choice to steal the blessing of shared resources made abundantly available by God the Provider. The desire here is to usurp and monopolize the rights to things already established, shared, or claimed by those other than oneself; to superimpose one's own stamp of ownership over the imprint of those who hold the same claim. **The evil in this desire is to choose to live the lie of SELF-INDULGENT PRIVILEGE.** Once again, sin.

Sin is not the catalogue of all the great big bad things we choose to do—nor even a listing of the far more numerous little bad things we choose to do; SIN IS THE FACT THAT EVERY DESIRE OF OUR HEARTS, EVERY THOUGHT OF OUR MINDS, AND EVERY DYING FIBER OF OUR BODIES FALLS SHORT OF GOD'S MINIMUM DESIGN STANDARDS! We are out of order. Intended laws do not apply. What is conceived when any human is born is a life departed from its created norm, already engulfed in the lawlessness called *SIN* . . . **that all-consuming malady of fatal shortcomings and selfish desires.** We are a failing race of people.

> "The LORD looks down from heaven on the sons of men to see if there are any who understand, any who seek God. All have turned aside, they have together become corrupt; there is no one who does good, not even one."
>
> (Psalm 14: 2, 3)

We are all in this together because—from the first human who ever became untrue to God's perfect design, to our very own children's children—this affliction has passed along unchecked throughout generations:

> "Behold, I was brought forth in [a state of] iniquity; my mother was sinful who conceived me [and I too am sinful]."
>
> (Psalm 51:5; The Amplified Bible)

Where does the pattern for an untrue nature originate from in the first place?? It certainly could not come from God. The Bible indicates that the character of God is so true, even the words of God do not fail or become empty (**Luke 16:17**). But the Bible also reveals the original source of untruthfulness—and the pattern for every human life that has manifested PRIDE-posturing, INDEPENDENCE-proclaiming, and PRIVILEGE- pocketing lies:

> "You belong to your father, the devil, and you want to carry out your father's desire. He was a murderer from the beginning, not holding to truth, for there is no truth in him. When he lies, he speaks his native language, for he is a liar and the father of lies."
>
> (John 8: 44)

> "[But] he who commits sin [who practices evildoing] is of the devil [takes his character from the evil one], for the devil has sinned (violated the divine law) from the beginning."

71

(1 John 3: 9; The Amplified Bible)

If we do inherit our failing character from a devil who is also called the father of lies, then we have just further confirmed that we die, because, by nature, we are born in the *UNTRUE* character of a father figure few would admit to. We are not as we were meant to be! But wait just a minute . . .

"SPECIAL OFFER, FOLKS"

Step right up!! God has an offer just for you today . . . an extraordinarily special offer. This value *cannot* be beat—because its already been purchased by God Himself! It's all stored up right now, in heavenly storehouses, ready to literally be *GIVEN* away!!! Today is the day, folks! You, or anyone else who wants to, can take advantage of God's once-in-a-lifetime extraordinarily special offer! I absolutely guarantee no matter where you search, you won't find an opportunity like this *anywhere else* in the universe!! LIMITED TIME ONLY! Step right up before this offer is no longer available! Step right up—the choice is yours! Take it or leave it, folks . . . but if you decide to leave it, you're going to find out real fast that sin stains badly, and those kind of stains don't come out without a *whole* lot of help! You can't get sin out on your own—cleaning out sin takes the kind of resources that money just can't buy!!

Just imagine yourself as a beautiful tailor-made shirt or blouse, but right from the start you've gotten stained with a terrible stinking kind of red stain that was eating you up thread by thread. You could wring yourself out . . . tie yourself in knots . . . beat yourself against the rocks . . . only to find out that because you're dragging around on only *THE* most polluted planet in the universe, the stains are spreading, folks, to places you didn't even know were there! Maybe you realize the truth in the Bible verse:

"All of us have become like one who is unclean, and all our righteous acts are like filthy rags . . ."

(Isaiah 64:6)

In other words, folks, we're really messed up, and most of us are kidding ourselves straight to the incinerator. We wear out slowly like the stained articles of clothing you wash and wash—but all they do is fade . . . and they *never* come clean. We've lost just about all of our bright colors and we're living faded, blotted lives; the sin stains keep right on spreading, my friends. So, this is what God is offering:

> "'Come now, let us reason together,' says the LORD. 'Though your sins are like scarlet, they shall be as white as snow; though they are red like crimson, they shall be like wool.'"
>
> (Isaiah 1:18)

Basically God is saying, "Wise up! Billions of people have tried . . . and failed . . . to raise their standards to My level. Messed-up human beings aren't large enough to clean up their own act to My satisfaction. You've got to be perfect if we're gonna be tight—and it's impossible for anyone as imperfect as *all* of you have become to even understand what it takes to live a pure life anymore."

"So it's gonna have to be Me who saves you. I'm the only perfect one you know—so I'm gonna have to be the one to jumpstart you over to My kind of living. It's not my right to *force* you to get it right; that's a choice I leave to you. But I'm making Myself available, if you want me. I'm offering you the best solution there is . . . ME. **I AM LIFE ITSELF.** Subtract even the littlest bit of LIFE, and all you've got left in its place is a bit of death . . . as I'm sure you know from personal experience. But I'd love to change all of that 'dying' nonsense. For good. All you have to do is put your little hands in mine, relax, and let me do the work!"

Well, by now I'm sure you're asking, "What work is God gonna do for me?" Folks, we call His offer, **The Great Exchange.**

> God made him who had no sin to be sin for us, so that in him we might become the righteousness of God.
>
> (2 Corinthians 5:21)

Who's "him," you ask? Think about it, folks. How many "hims" do you know of who have no sin? The only one I know of is God Himself! In fact, only somebody as infinite as God could possibly have the capacity to—in one great act—make it possible to clean away the stains of everyone ever born! And only God has the ability to offer to place forever into our lives His own righteous living . . . in return for letting Him take away our dead and dirty living. **What an incredible opportunity, folks!** That God would offer to live inside of us all that righteous living, so that we no longer have to try at doing what we know is impossible for us to do! All that anyone needs to do is let Him in to fill up your life!

Now, I can already hear some of you saying, "How is somebody as big as God going to fit into my little tiny life unless he makes Himself small enough not to obliterate me in the process?" Good question, ladies and gentlemen! The answer is: HE DID!! God allowed a part of Himself to become as small as a man, so that there would exist a bridge to connect to all of humanity on one end . . . and to all of Himself on the other; a pipeline through which you can have the worst of your sins sucked right away—and through which you can receive into your life the presence of our perfect God! That part of God's Person that He shrunk-to-fit. He placed His Life right in the gap between God and man . . . that jumper cable from His revved up Perfection to ignite life into the cold engine of our imperfection . . . THAT WAS THE LIFE OF JESUS CHRIST:

> **"Your attitude should be the same as that of Christ Jesus: Who, being in very nature God, did not consider equality with God something to be grasped, but made himself nothing, taking the very nature of a servant, being found in appearance as a man, he humbled himself and became obedient to death—even death on a cross! Therefore God exalted him to the highest place and gave him the name above every name, that at the name of Jesus every knee should bow, in heaven and on earth and under the earth, and every tongue confess that Jesus Christ is Lord, to the glory of God the Father."**
> **(Philippians 2:5–11)**

Listen to what happened to me, folks. It was at the cross that the stretch from God to a wretch like me was completed. By taking upon his very important life *all* the mess of my sin, and sacrificing Himself to die the death my sins had doomed me to, Jesus Christ opened up a doorway for me to get together with a Holy God who by nature must destroy all things stained with sin.

Suddenly there wasn't a sinful thing blocking the way between me and God!! Suddenly I was able to hand over to Him the *whole* terrible burden of my natural-born destiny! Suddenly, because of Jesus being raised from the dead, the door he had opened for us to touch God was ripped from its hinges and opened to stay! Suddenly God could put into my hands the *whole* wonderful gift of Christ's born-again destiny! **Jesus Christ took my awful destiny because of God's love . . . and then He conquered it! Jesus Christ won His glorious destiny because of His sacrifice . . . and now he's sharing it!**

So folks, I say again, step right up! This is a grand offer, folks! But remember, it's strictly for a limited time only! Already bought and paid for by the Almighty God Himself—and ready to be handed right over to you at the moment you step on out of that crowd to let God know you want what He has for you! All you have to do is ask, and you've got **The Great Exchange: trade in your personal sinfulness . . . and receive the personal Righteousness of Jesus Christ in return!!** Then after you've tried and seen the change in your life, and know that His offer is good, please take time to make the sacrifice to share your new life around. Let your family and friends get in on this extraordinarily special offer. Let God take special care of you . . . while the offer still lasts!

> **"For since death came through a man, the resurrection of the dead comes also through a man. For as in Adam all die, so in Christ all will be made alive."**
>
> (1 Corinthians 15:21, 22)

STOP AND THINK.

If I have fallen and I can't get up . . .
I need to accept a helping hand.
But I will only grasp that hand with all my remaining strength
if I believe that helping hand is strong enough to lift me.

LIVE A LIFE WORTH GIVING.

Part 2.

"... OFFER YOUR BODIES AS LIVING SACRIFICES, HOLY AND PLEASING TO GOD ... DO NOT CONFORM ANY LONGER TO THE PATTERN OF THIS WORLD, BUT BE TRANSFORMED BY THE RENEWING OF YOUR MIND."

STARTING OVER

A special joy abounds inside me
'cause I'm leaving sin behind me;
whatever it is that I was then
just died.
I'm starting up my life again.
Christ just came in . . .
I'm new in Him.

Leavin' all that stuff behind
    it held me back
    it weighed me down
But Christ has turned my life around
    He stripped me clean
    He washed me down
Became the Master of my heart
    He saw the sin
    He threw it out
Gave me the chance to live again
    He shed my corpse
    and gave me wings . . .

So now I'm soaring in His Spirit;
His life rising through my spirit.
Energy from up above!
Starting over . . .
through His love.

Chapter 5

New Perspectives

Forget the former things; do not dwell on the past. See, I am doing a new thing! Now it springs up; do you not perceive it?

(The Word of God in Isaiah 43:18, 19)

I was never much of a conformist. Perhaps this fact was my lone source of self-esteem. While still in grade school, my male classmates would regularly come together at recess to play a game of punchball in the schoolyard. I would not join them. In fact, I really wasn't interested. More interesting to me was sitting alone by the fence under the big oak trees—folding dead leaves into imaginary spaceships.

But I've since learned how conformed to the lives of my schoolmates my life actually was. It was a fact that my life was just as devoid of the knowledge of the presence of God as was theirs! Public School 52 was conforming us . . . our families were conforming us . . . and we were conforming each other to a life incompatible with the interests or influence of God. Humans, by nature, will always conform to one thing or another.

By now, we have seen God's mercy. We saw it in His willingness to offer so great a salvation. We have tasted it and touched it, and know we know it is present with us. The God of this universe desires to reunite us to Himself, despite our alienated and unbalanced condition. But there is a problem. Medicine reveals that when a foreign body is newly grafted into a host organism, it will be rejected as hostile, invading tissue. That is the natural course of things. Whether it be a new heart or a new kidney, incompatible tissue endangers the whole body, causing a violent purging reaction that threatens all health. The host is forced to destroy the troublesome new organ quickly in order to prevent "contamination." This cannot be allowed, from a healer's point of view. Preventive measures must be taken that will make such an occurrence the most remote possibility—injections of anti-rejection medications. The host organism must be made to find the newly grafted organ a compatible partner in living!

IF WE REMAIN CONFORMED TO THE PATTERN OF THIS CORRUPTED WORLD, WE WILL FIND OURSELVES AT ODDS WITH THE CREATOR OF A PERFECT UNIVERSE. No contest. We're the ones who will lose out. If we are to find ourselves at home in this new place of living we now may choose to be lifted to, we have to decide that we're ready to be conformed, transplanted, and transformed to a truly new way of life. To illustrate, I offer a series of parables.

A Biblical Point of View

We have already established that sin begins purely as a personal malady. In fact, the Bible openly reveals for us the circumstances of how sin was first allowed a home in the heart of the first adversary to God's principles of Life, Light, and Love. Revelation about this person comes within a prophecy delivered by the Hebrew prophet Ezekiel against the then-enthroned "prince" of the "wicked" kingdom of Tyre; a second person, with a far distant beginning is at the same time being addressed here. The implication is that this unseen being, obviously more than an imperfect man, is the actual power behind the prince's reign:

> "The word of the LORD came to me: "Son of man, take up a lament concerning the king of Tyre and say to him: `This is what the Sovereign LORD says: "You were the model of perfection, full of wisdom

and perfect in beauty. You were in Eden, the garden of God; every precious stone adorned you: ruby, topaz and emerald, chrysolite, onyx and jasper, sapphire, turquoise and beryl. Your settings and mountings were made of gold; on the day you were created they were prepared. You were anointed as a guardian cherub, for so I ordained you. You were blameless in your ways from the day you were created till wickedness was found in you. Through your wide-spread trade you were filled with violence and you sinned . . ."

(Ezekiel 28:11–16)

Within the heart of the adversary to God spoken of here we see the first terrible conception of sin. Before that moment stretched an immeasurable period of time when Truth and Perfection was all that there was. Wrongdoing was not conceivable. **What was the catalyst that gave birth to wrongdoing?** What corruption took place in the heart of this person that made him lead a violent assault against Truth?? Our answer is found in a grieving lament as communicated by God through His prophet Isaiah in a prophecy against an ancient king of Babylon—and also against someone else, obviously more than an earthbound man:

"How you have fallen from heaven, O morning star, son of the dawn! You have been cast down to the earth, you who once laid low the nations! You said in your heart, 'I will ascend to heaven; I will raise my throne above the stars of God; I will sit enthroned on the mount of the assembly, on the utmost heights of the sacred mountain. I will ascend above the tops of the clouds; I will make myself like the Most High.'"

(Isaiah 14:12–14)

What do these words reveal to us of the origin of sin? Our investigation so far tips us to several conclusions. That it grew out of an individual's personal choice . . . a decision to oppose what had always been good . . . a decision to contest what had always been steadfast . . . a decision to tear away from the only source of Life, Light and Love. **In short, it was the deliberate choice to section off a territory of living entirely out of touch with authenticity—an ingenuine existence. A condition of false-**

hood. *THE FIRST LIE*. All was lost. The morning star was emptied of his true nature. In essence he became:

A DECOMPOSED carcass after the evacuation of LIFE.

A DARK absence after the evacuation of LIGHT.

A DESECRATED waste after the evacuation of LOVE.

SIN had entered the universe through one individual's bad choice; its spread would be a person-to-person epidemic. In the previous biblical description of the state of this fallen one's heart, we see the familiar pattern of lies: We see the posture of SELF-IMPORTANCE; we hear the defiance of SELF-RELIANCE; we feel the grab of SELF-INDULGENCE. This was open rebellion. How did God respond to this personal attack??

> **"Your heart became proud on account of your beauty, and you corrupted your wisdom because of your splendor. So I threw you to earth . . ."**
>
> **(Ezekiel 28:17)**

> **"Then war broke out in heaven; Michael and his angels went forth to battle with the dragon, and the dragon and his angels fought. But there was no room found for them in heaven any longer. And the huge dragon was cast down *and* out—that age-old serpent, who is called the Devil and Satan, he who is the seducer (deceiver) of all humanity the world over; he was forced out *and* down to the earth, and his angels were flung out along with him."**
>
> **(Revelation 12:7–9; The Amplified Bible)**

Life vs. Decomposition. Light vs. Darkness. Love vs. Desecration. *HOLINESS vs. SIN*. None of these opposites can occupy the same space at the same time. They repel each other. They disrupt each other's existence. God and all created things still true to themselves, by nature, could never topple or fall. For in a conflict between the false and true, it is the lie—which is without foundation—that eventually gives way! The Bible says that the Devil and his rebel followers were flung to earth—but when they hit ground they were to find that the Earth and all therein had been entrusted to the care of a new kind of being. Human beings with the privilege to oversee and manage the planet as they chose to, and benefit from it to their good pleasure.

"So God created man in his own image, in the image of God he created him; male and female he created them. God blessed them and said to them, "Be fruitful and increase in number; fill the earth and subdue it. Rule over the fish of the sea and the birds of the air and over every living creature that moves on the ground."

(Genesis 1:27,28)

Well, the Devil wasn't having this. What he found on Earth was filled with the goodness of God and all of His holy authority. And that fact alone made it inevitable that Satan would kick up his heels again! Satan wanted to be glorified as God—master of the universe. *Yet Satan could no more compare with the God he'd forsaken than any creation could ever assume the place of its Creator!* Yet if God could not be overthrown as Master of the Universe, Satan would settle for toppling Humanity and becoming Master of the Earth. But since no one but God can call what does not exist into being, the Devil was extremely limited as to how to make the Earth over to his illegitimate liking.

Unable to remake Earth, the Devil took up the subtle art of Corruption; he could take plump red apples gleaming in the sunlight, shrivel them brown and infect them with rot! **Vandalism and Counterfeiting would be the means to his end.** He would work to obscure, to erase, to blot over, to burn, to trash, and rip apart all the signatures (pure Life, Light, and Love) that identify anyone or anything as God's handiwork. Then he would scrawl his personal trademarks (utter Decay, Darkness, and Desecration) over every surface visible to the earthly eye, and pass off these counterfeits as the stuff life is made of!

But before Satan could begin his sick agenda, he first felt compelled to acquire the Earth as his own and apparently rightful possession. Why go through the trouble? Why not just attack and destroy? Because Satan knew he would never accomplish his goal if he appeared as insane as he is. **His goal, remember, is to have the highest seat and to be both worshipped and obeyed, even if by default.**

He was aware that he had to *seduce* intelligent beings into trusting and believing in the path of selfish independence as superior to the path of obedience to God. Therefore, Satan knew that he needed to appear to be beautiful, brilliant, on-the-level, easy to please, and easy to follow.

Once he had, through the bedazzlement of deception, won the deluded following that he so desired . . . then and only then would his *fun* begin.

So the first act of the Devil on Earth was to tell a lie. The first purpose of that lie would be to steal what was given to humankind and make the Earth as his own. Satan is shrewd and powerful enough to take advantage of anyone who makes a choice to stand alone apart from the all-powerful care of God. So he approached the innocent Adam and Eve, human caretakers of God's green Earth, and presented them with a lie to coax them into making this choice.

Satan was aware that God enjoyed a uniquely close relationship with these new human beings, that He trusted them to superintend the planet, free to make choices as they saw fit. But God also carefully instructed them to stay away from the fruit of one particular tree out of the thousands Adam and Eve had at their disposal in the garden called Eden. This was no hardship; the warning was simply meant to keep them alive and well.

The day Adam and Eve exposed themselves to an intimate knowledge of both "good *and* evil" . . . the day they chose to go their own way, separating from the protecting command and sovereign authority of their God and Father, they would find all connection to Him ruptured. They would be isolated from their Supply of pure Life, Light, and Love, and thus doomed to "surely die!" **(Genesis 2:16,17)** So what Satan did first was to plant confusion by obscuring God's warning with the question,

> **"Can it really be that God has said, 'You shall not eat from every tree of the garden?'"**
>
> **(Genesis 3:1; The Amplified Bible)**

Satan knew exactly what God had said. But after manipulating God's words in the memory of the unsuspecting humans, he then presented them his own bold-faced lie. A stupendous lie. A lie designed to persuade the humans into freely choosing to act Self-importantly, Self-reliantly, and Self-indulgently against their Father's good nature. Satan said to them,

"You will not surely die, for God knows that when you eat of it your eyes will be opened, and you will be like God, knowing good and evil."

(Genesis 3:4, 5)

Convinced by this verbal maneuvering, the humans ate from the tree. And in one great stroke they cut themselves off from Father and Function, Source and Sustenance, and the Important Living they had exercised while having dominion over the planet. What had taken place? IN A MOST CUNNING MANNER, SATAN HAD GIVEN THE HUMAN BEINGS A DIRECTIVE TO FOLLOW. ADAM AND EVE KNEW VERY WELL WHOSE LEAD THEY WERE SOLELY DEVOTED TO FOLLOW: THE HOLY ONE WHO BROUGHT THEM INTO BEING, WHO IN-STALLED THEM AS THE SOLE CARETAKERS OF THE EARTH . . . THE ONE WHO WAS PROVEN TRUE. **BUT THEY LISTENED IN-STEAD TO A STRANGER'S INSTRUCTION—AND THEN ACTED IN ACCORDANCE WITH HIS UNTESTED GUIDANCE!** But wait. It actually gets worse.

The deeper tragedy was that Satan had illegitimately positioned himself in the midst of human affairs as a subverting authority. Not thinking, Adam and Eve counted this stranger's judgment as more valid than their own. Even though their Heavenly Father delegated to them authority and dominion over the affairs of the Earth, they deferred to Satan. In a foolish moment, they surrendered their charge to look after the best interests of the planet and subjected themselves to the will of the stranger in their garden.

The consequences of Adam and Eve's decision left Humanity stripped "naked" of true Life, true Light, and true Love. **And the stranger called Satan now held claim to dominion over the earth.** He wasn't about to give it back. With this license in hand he would take advantage of the opportunity to pervert the entire face of the earth and everything therein. According to the Bible:

". . . the whole world is under the control of the evil one."

(1 John 5:19)

85

As the king goes, so goes the kingdom. The problem for the Earth is that Satan is going to Hell. This leaves the Earth's inhabitants in a dreadful situation. Nothing our natural senses perceive is true to itself.

Life, like a garden, is meant to grow and flourish, yet can end up decaying in a reeking compost heap instead.

Light, like the sun's rays, is to color, shape, and warm, yet it flickers and dies out at the end of each day.

Love, like a faithful friend, is to ever stand by our side; yet we are all too familiar with desecration of abandonment and betrayal.

The unreliability of the *counterfeit* has been brought to all we perceive with the five physical senses. Everything seen, heard, smelled, tasted, or touched eventually obscures, discolors, fades, or suddenly explodes. All that we hope for coughs a last breath, sings a final song, moans a mortal cry, loses its perfume, ends up stinking rotten, exhausts all of its flavor, turns stale, becomes spoiled, and decomposes. In the course of time, every living thing dies; every energy diminishes; every structure becomes unstable; every object erodes; every liquid evaporates; every memory becomes vague; every vapor dissipates! Things fall apart. The ending of a thing is as certain, as it is without mercy, as it is all-devouring . . . as it is without redemption.

And what is such finality but the utmost transgression against an immortal, eternal Creator! It is a deviation from the plans of the One who desires for all of Creation to live, to grow, and magnify for time without end. There is a consequence here; it is unavoidable. We who choose to remain in sin . . . to remain parted from the true and the good . . . to live in the fatal manner we've thus far barely survived . . . must embrace a logical result:

SIN = a consequence of untrue living and a separation from **GOD**
GOD = **LIFE**
SIN = a consequence of untrue living and a separation from **LIFE**
SIN = **DEATH**

What is a body then to do? What hope is there for us to have? Left to ourselves, it would seem we'd have little choice but to join our voices in despairing lament with the ancient Hebrew teacher Ezra, who long ago grieved:

> "O my God, I am too ashamed and disgraced to lift up my face to you, my God, because our sins are higher than our heads and our guilt has reached the heavens."
>
> (Ezra 9:6)

How does our God respond to our suffocating outcry? Is it His intention to treat us as if we were an unfortunate mistake in His judgment, best quickly crushed in hand and tossed in the heavenly wastebasket? No. A perfect being does not make unfortunate mistakes in judgment. We were each made for great and important reasons—and we were made with the free will to choose to live them out! After all, we were especially made in His image—before we chose to conform instead to the personality of the Adversary so dead set against Him.

Then will God allow us to thrash about in our filth just to punish us and make an example of us for daring to reject Him?? No. No matter how foolish we choose to be, He cannot change His desire to correct us. Though He cannot tolerate corruption, His compassion cannot fail!

No. He has given us this hope: *HE HAS OFFERED US HIMSELF.* HE HAS OFFERED TO PLACE HIMSELF, IN ALL OF HIS INFINITY, FOREVER BETWEEN OUR SINS AND OUR SELVES—TO SEPARATE US SO IMMEASURABLY FAR FROM OUR SIN, THAT OUR SIN WILL NO LONGER BE SEEN IN CONNECTION TO US!

To save us from the consequences of our wretched condition, God has extended to us the total force of His character. According to the Truth revealed in the Bible, our Father has reached way down to save us as we, in our state of weakness, reach up to accept His mighty hand, and the forgiving grace of His nature:

> "The LORD is compassionate and gracious, slow to anger, abounding in love. He will not always accuse, nor will he harbor his anger forever; he does not treat us as our sins deserve or repay according to our iniquities. For as high as the heavens are above the earth, so

great is his love for those that fear him; as far as the east is from the west, so far has he removed our transgressions from us."

(Psalm 103:8–12)

A CATERPILLAR'S POINT OF VIEW

Y'now, you and I are taught to misunderstand what comes as easily as breathing . . . the end of breathing.

And what you and I don't understand, we fear.

So you and I learn to fear it, and therefore not to think about it, certainly not to talk about, and to never even hear of it . . . death, that is. Although you and I at this very moment are dying.

True, you and the person sitting or standing nearest to you are living at approximately 98.6 degrees warm . . . at the moment. But given just a little bit of time in the grand scheme of things, you or I, or the he or she sitting or standing nearest to you will suddenly be laying . . . stiffened and cold to the touch. You can't deny it. BOTH LIFE AND DEATH ARE EQUALLY WITHIN OUR REACH RIGHT NOW. Between every breath we take, there is a momentary end of breathing. Between every heart-beat . . . there is a pause.

I'm talking about life. I'm talking about death. You can turn up the noise and pump up the volume if you don't want to think about it, talk about it, or hear about it—but you *will* experience it. When? Soon enough. Let's just say the countdown is already started!

Hey, WAIT! Before you walk away in disgust, let me ask you an off-the-wall kind of question. When was the last time you thought or talked or heard about the life and death of a caterpillar? I am *not* talking about the untimely type of caterpillar death, where it ends up squished across the bottom of a six-year-old's sneaker! No. I'm talking about that natural cycle of existence to which every green-blooded, civilized caterpillar aspires. That cycle of existence that begins with life, ends with death, and then . . . well, I'll get to that in a moment.

BUT SINCE I'VE GOT YOUR ATTENTION, consider this. Do you think caterpillars are as afraid of dying as humans can't seem to help being? Not a chance! As a matter of fact, caterpillars *embrace* death— and you would too if you had to live your life from a caterpillar's point of view! Picture yourself . . . crawling through mud and grass and weeds so thick, it's impossible to know where you are going . . . getting trapped on the outermost twigs of branches swaying in trouble-making breezes . . . endlessly chewing and chewing and chewing on the foulest, most nauseating leaves, yet never being able to get filled up on the stuff . . . maneuvering slowly around the clumps of excrement some big dumb animal nearly dumps on you . . . a lot of bird-watching . . . a lot *more* bird-watching. Evading that six-year-old named Nathaniel. Then realizing to your horror that there are *thousands* of other six-year-olds out there—and that they all wear incredibly large sneakers! Well then, you might finally sense the outright enthusiasm of a caterpillar when it's *FINALLY* time to die.

It finds a tiny, private place and secludes itself in a cocoon—a cocoon that seals it off from awareness of all danger, distraction, and stress. And in that place it fully surrenders to the death of all it has ever known, ever suffered through, ever been. And in giving up its mundane, crawl-around-in-the-dirt existence, suddenly the caterpillar's acceptance of death also invites a transformation! From within, it is resurrected, unfolding into a new life no caterpillar could conceive of. In the laying down of what once was, a new birth is allowed to take place. First caterpillar life, then the laying down of that life, then a new birth into . . . you know . . . BUTTERFLY LIFE!

Have you ever really watched a butterfly? Watched the winds come up beneath them, carrying them up into the sunlight hundreds of feet above the only existence they had ever before known—to survey the world from a point of view never before seen—to be held aloft on sculpted wings never before possessed, each arrayed in an individual splendor not quite like that of any other butterfly! If you've watched as butterflies glide and flutter, or watched as they drink the sweet nectar of flowers, or watched them spin in new-found freedom safely above little Nathaniel's big head—then perhaps you can see why a butterfly always seems to be dancing a celebration of praise! The old caterpillar has been laid to rest, and something new raised to life in its place.

> "But someone will say, "How can the dead be raised? With what [kind of] body will they come forth?" You foolish man! Every time you plant seed, you sow something that does not come to life [germinating, springing up and growing] unless it dies first . . . But God gives to it the body He plans *and* sees fit, and to each kind of seed a body of its own."
>
> (1 Corinthians 15:35, 36, 38; The Amplified Bible)

In other words, *the caterpillar is just the seed that God has made for growing the butterfly!* This fact is important, especially depending on how you answer some of these questions: Ever felt like the progression of your life was moving at . . . oh, a caterpillar's pace? Have you ever felt like you were "stuck in the mud?" Do you find it almost an impossible task to know where your life is going next? Ever find yourself trapped way out on a limb, totally unable to brace yourself against the ill winds that rock your life? Fed up with the same old unpleasantness—yet unable to give it up because of cravings you can't ever fill? Constantly getting dumped on? Scared of being gobbled up one day by any of life's many dangers?

DOESN'T THIS SOUND A LOT LIKE A CATERPILLAR'S WAY OF LIFE? But hold on! We have discovered that no matter how lowly a life we now lead, it can . . . it *must* . . . be sacrificed that we might be born-again. Remember the caterpillar?

A caterpillar enters the darkness of the cocoon, gives itself to death, and there emerges a fluttering butterfly. A sperm enters the darkness of an egg, gives itself to death, and there emerges an offspring. A seed kernel enters the darkness of the soil, gives itself to death, and there emerges a seedling. Jesus Christ entered the darkness of God's punishment for sin, gave himself to death, and there emerged The Anointed Savior—called King of Kings and Lord of Lords!

And what of us? Into what darkness must *we* enter?

"Now it is an extraordinary thing for one to give his life even for an upright man, though perhaps for a noble *and* lovable *and* generous benefactor someone might even dare die. But God shows and clearly proves His [own] love for us by the fact that while we were still sinners, Christ (the Messiah, the Anointed One) died for us."
(Romans 5:6–8; The Amplified Bible)

A friend gave His life to save our eternal souls. No darker day has there ever been than the day the Son of God was condemned and slain—for a guilt that wasn't His own. The guilt was mine. It was yours. The day we acknowledge that Christ died in our place is the day we realize our share in His death. He died our death, yet He had no fault. We are implicated in the death of an innocent. That is our darkness. Yet if we desire new life, it is here we must enter! IF WE SEEK OUR FULFILL-MENT, THEN LIKE OUR FRIEND JESUS, WE MUST DIE.

Just before He was taken captive, Christ was overheard by His disciples expressing to God the Father His willingness to die; he said, ". . . not my will, but yours be done" (Luke 22:42). If we desire new life, then along with Christ, in the same way *we* must die—die to the preservation of SELF . . . die to the plans we've mapped out for our lives . . . die to life as we've always known it. Just like the caterpillar. Embracing the transformation that God has planned us for! Taking on the new lifestyle we've been fashioned to fit! ONLY THEN SHALL WE EMERGE FROM THE DARKNESS, LIKE OUR SAVIOR JESUS CHRIST, AND FLY . . .

". . . because anyone who has died has been freed from sin. Now if we died with Christ, we believe that we will also live with him. For we know that since Christ was raised from the dead, he cannot die again; death no longer has mastery over him. The death he died, he died to sin once for all; but the life he lives, he lives to God. In the same way count yourselves dead to sin, but alive to God in Christ Jesus."
(Romans 6:7–11)

A Savior's Point of View

Listen to the heart of the Savior:

I am the River. I am refreshing and free. I have run the course from tragedy to glory. I have been touched by violent pollution, yet the vastness of my flow has swept even my deepest undercurrents utterly clean.

In the beginning, every delightful globule of effervescence I conceived was destined to be weightless, shimmering, and transparent . . . swirling freely within my life-giving waters. Each would be one of a countless number, transported in a vast sparkling fellowship as I flowed swiftly toward an ocean of glory ahead. But the churning bubbles became attracted to what was beneath me. As soon as any bubble came into contact with the mud beneath me, a muddy film developed that ran across and adhered to its surface, keeping it from breaking free. And every delicate globule that was tempted to rub "shoulders" with the growing numbers of grounded companions, found itself also quite stuck.

Rather than holding to what they knew was good—the warmth of the sunlight filtering in from above . . . the greatness of the ocean just ahead . . . the uncontaminated waters that had always carried them—the attraction instead was to the mud beneath. The result was tragic. Not a single bubble remained in the purity of my effervescence. The mire that sprang from the mud, entrapping them, hardened quickly into a casing—effectively imbedding each bubble in the earth's sediment!

Billions of the mired bubbles now could no longer rise to rejoin the flow of the river. In the mud, they became acquainted with pollution. Swallowed in mud, the mud became their ceiling. Many could still sense the immense stirrings of my Living Waters rushing above them, but "out of sight" meant "out of mind," and they could no longer imagine being in touch with such immensity. Many others had become so terribly encrusted, they could no longer sense my movement above—they therefore proclaimed that mud was all there was. Within their diminished pockets of existence, the mud suffocated everything with a stagnant impurity.

There were countless clusters of these blister-shaped imprisonments . . . yet because each globule was individually encased, even though there was a common proximity, there was never again the full fellowship bubbles were designed for. And even if they *could* truly touch each other, each was out of touch with the original environment meant to carry along their movements; and now they were evaporating; now they were depleted; now they were thick and without transparency; some were no more than emptied cavities. Fossils of what once was.

I am the River. My love for those who once lived in me, who now live far beneath me, is ever undiminished. It is for that reason I take action in a manner only I can fully comprehend. I take the essence of my power and freedom—the freshness on my running waters in all its infinite purity—and invest it into the form of a perfect globule exactly like that of the billions below! As a free-spirited bubble, I have placed myself into the lower parts of the earth's crust . . . YET MY PURITY REPELS ALL POLLUTION!

A few of these mud-dwellers on whom I have had pity believed help would come one day—but they expected their Deliverer to come from within their immobile ranks. A shimmering and transparent bubble, unsoiled by the mud, I am absolutely unfathomable to their understanding. Before long, I will be assaulted and brutally crushed by those lost beneath the mud. Yet in what they believe to by my brokenness, I will become their Savior. **I am pure; therefore the mud *cannot* hold me. I will part its lifeless sediment; I will arise from beneath its weight; I will shatter the earth's crust carrying bubbles once held captive in my train as we dance together toward the sun-drenched surface.** Those formerly imprisoned, who make the most of this opportunity, will attach themselves to me; they will be flushed clean by the immensity of my purity; they will be lifted again, free spirits transported in the power of my currents and eddies!

I am the River. I am refreshing and free. I have run the course from tragedy to glory. I have been touched by violent pollution, yet the vastness of my flow has swept even my deepest currents utterly clean. I approach the ocean. Come taste and see that I am good!

A CREATOR'S POINT OF VIEW

Put yourself in God's perfect shoes for a moment. You designed this perfect masterpiece of a creation with the ability to think logically, weigh options, and make creative choices . . . just like You. Made in them in Your image. Named them "Humans." Good job, You said. And You installed them as a vital organ in the infinite body of Your entire Creation . . . in a position to generate life. These humans, so close to Your very heart, became the "Heart" of Your whole operation. But as God, You alone are the amazing "Brain."

This "Heart" concluded rather quickly that it was too important to be only a part of the operation! So it decided to cut loose. Of course, it landed on the ground. It sloshed about, unable to do what it was designed to do, gushing away its resources, making an absolute mess. It got filthy, covered in dirt and all sorts of filth.

Traumatized, damaged, massively infected, the organ began to rapidly die. And the life of the entire immortal body of Your Creation was horribly wounded as well! This dying "Heart" could never be returned to its original place in such a state of dysfunction and failure. The body of Creation would only reject it in a major attack by its protective immune system—**it's holy perfection.** This immune system attacks anything less than holy and perfect as a threat to the body. The threat is contained and destroyed.

But You are the Creator . . . this is Your masterpiece . . . and You value this Humanity with a love beyond their ability to know or measure. For You have invested into their being the wealth of Your infinite resources. YOU WANT THEM BACK . . . *YOU WANT EVERY HUMAN BEING—EVERY LAST CELL OF THIS "HEART" BACK IN ITS PLACE!*

> "Like water spilled on the ground, which cannot be recovered, so we must die. But God does not take away life; instead, he devises ways so that a banished person may not remain estranged from him."
> (2 Samuel 14:14)

You will direct aid to your "Heart"—one cell at a time! For every one of a trillion struggling "Heart cells" you will make a way so that any who might desire a way out on a bad decision—a way back up to the place where they rightfully belong—might first be cleansed of infection and injury. The "Heart" convulsed and contorted with its efforts to lift itself up off the ground. Some of its cells and chambers send up this heartfelt cry:

> **"We are brought down to the dust; our bodies cling to the ground. Rise up and help us; redeem us because of your unfailing love."**
> **(Psalm 44:25,26)**

So You who alone are God prepared one new and perfect "Heart cell" to be transplanted right in the center of the ebbing life of the dismembered and failing heart. A clean and uninfected "heart cell" absolutely true to the "Heart's" original design—for when entering the "Heart of Death," only that which is true could resurrect itself!

But here is the crux of the matter: in order for this single perfect cell to be the means for disinfecting and restoring every one of the infected cells, it had to have the capacity to intimately interact with a trillion cells at a time. YET ONLY THE BRAIN HAS SUCH A LIMITLESS CAPACITY TO CONNECT SIMULTANEOUSLY WITH EVERY CELL OF ITS BODY. Therefore, in order to fulfill its calling, this perfect cell had to be fully Brain, as well as fully Heart—fully God, as well as fully Human. So You made Him a special creation; a Savior. As many as would touch and cling to Him, this Savior would decontaminate in a free exchange of His purity.

> **"But you know that he appeared so that he might take away our sins. And in him is no sin."**
> **(1 John 3:5)**

So, Christ entered the "Heart of Death" (as only a mortal human has the capacity to do) to permanently connect with and end the dying of uncounted numbers of human "cells" (as only Almighty God has the capacity to do). Then You as Creator lifted this Savior from the death that had momentarily enfolded Him—and You installed this Christ as the new Heart of the body of Your Creation! And lifted up along with this Christ came all who allowed Him to take hold of their failure and raise them also from Death to Newness. The power of this Christ was the power to save! His attachment to Humanity's failed condition became Your chosen vehicle to carry them back to the heights from which they had fallen!

> ". . . I, when I am lifted up from the earth, will draw all men to myself."
>
> (John 12:32)

Rising To The Occasion

Now, as the reader, you have the right to make a decision. Every day we make decisions—but the decision that has value is the one that is acted upon. This decision sets the course of your life. You can decide to accept God's offer of mercy as the answer to your need . . . and be lifted up in His direction. Or you can decide you'd be better off handling your own life . . . taking, as usual, your own direction.

My advice? Avail yourself to let God lift you up where you belong. Why die? Why remain trapped? Be born again. This is real, folks. Are you willing to call out Jesus Christ as the answer to your needs . . . and rise to the occasion of your salvation?

STOP AND THINK.

Anything can begin again
if the catalyst that originated life is initiated again.

A catalyst is necessary for summer, autumn, winter, or spring,
but the previous season first must end.

If I need new life, the wellspring will come from the Lifestream that
birthed me before.

LIVE A LIFE WORTH GIVING.

REJUVENATION

It bears witness to my weakness,
to my overwhelming smallness
in this vast expanding universe
that I have stood apart,
and that by living unconnected
to Important Living's Source
little life is left within me
death can hardly be resisted
strength reserves are all exhausted
bottomed out are my resources
insufficient are my options . . .

So I've decided to reconnect.

Important Living.
Re-beginning.
Open flow.
Newborn filling.
Death now ends.
Pure again.
I am transformed.
An infant learning,
new foods for new hunger yearnings:

Faith in God, now be my banquet.
Word of God, my nourishment.
Love served warm, my favorite portion.
And Holy Spirit,
sweet fresh Spirit,
forgiveness fountain,
quench my thirst!

Choosing To Cooperate: The End Of Self-Importance

<u>sacrifice</u> - the act of giving up one thing for another; destruction or surrender of something valued or desired for the sake of a higher object or more pressing claim.

(The World Book Dictionary)

Growing up, I loved to watch old black and white films on T.V. They had a character and a content totally unlike the newer movies of today. My favorite actor was James Cagney. I think it was because I perceived him to be a loner, a trait I was quite familiar with. But it was probably also because of my bias for "James" as a name.

One of the most powerful films I ever saw was a Cagney movie called "Angels with Dirty Faces." In it, Cagney plays a hardened gangster named Rocky. As the end of the film approaches, Rocky has been convicted of murder and is about to be taken to the electric chair. He's lost everything but his tough-guy pride, and that's a fame he's planning to take to his grave. He's a hero in the eyes of fellow death-row inmates and the adolescent gang members who roam the streets.

But Rocky's best buddy happens to have grown up to be a priest devoted to preventing those young gang members from ending up on death row as well. For that reason he asks Rocky to sacrifice his last possession . . . to sacrifice a tough-guy's pride . . . to be dragged to the electric chair weeping for mercy, sniveling, and begging not to die. Rocky is asked to do this so that some kids might stop idolizing his life as a gangster. Because Rocky had learned to care for a few of these kids, and because he had long cared for his childhood friend who had grown up to become a priest—and because he counted them all worth more than a tough guy's pride—Rocky, in the end, chooses to die as a coward.

In offering himself for his friend's saving cause, Rocky made the little that was left of his life an extension of a priestly work. By doing so, his life, for a moment, became invaluable to the priest. And then he was dead. He could do no more.

To offer your body as a living sacrifice to God is to make the whole of your being an instrument that is readily available at the reach of God's hand. In essence, it is to offer your self to serve as an extension of the Lord's reach into the midst of human affairs. This is confirmed when we see that "the Church"—those who make up God's worldwide fellow-ship of born-again creations—is called His Body. And a body is moved and directed from one center . . . the Brain. Indeed, Christ is identified as the "head" of the Body called "the Church" (**Colossians 1:18**).

If we understand how our own body is continually being offered to moment-by-moment unending instruction, impulse, and communica-tion from our own brain—and if we also understand the crippling effect upon a body that stops receiving major portions of the brain's instruc-tion and impulse, or the debilitating effect upon a body unable to deci-pher the messages the brain's electrical impulses—if we understand all this, then we understand that the offering of our bodies as living sacri-fices must mean:

1. an entire subordination to the instructions from above;
2. an effective connection so well tended and protected from erosion as to prevent any diminishment in the clarity of our reception;
3. and responses, so immediate, so involuntary, so automatic that we never run the risk of vital systems shutting down as our Head, Jesus Christ, transmits to us the input that keeps us healthily functioning from moment to moment.

Offering ourselves as living sacrifices is not a once-and-for-all act like Rocky's, but rather, *a constant activity*. Yet and still, when we take upon ourselves to act sacrificially, our living becomes efficient, movement never halting or stilted, the pounding of our pulse never skipping a beat. Our actions are timed in response to a higher control that moves us as fluidly as the runner who never alters a stride as he powers to the end of the race.

THE HARSH REALITY

Our behavior patterns are developed and reinforced by the consistency of our mental responses to the daily stimuli that are the context of our living. In other words, **our actions are the direct product of the patterns repeated in our very own thinking.** When we were living a life of independence, our will *alone* determined our activity. But to learn a life now dependent on a God who takes an active role in our living, means that it is necessary to *replace* our long-learned patterns of self-determined will and response.

We must reeducate ourselves to now respond first and primarily to a good and perfect will far higher than our own—a will so fair that it refuses to overpower or short-circuit the operation of our own wills. To make this decision demands a sacrifice. **That sacrifice is this:** *to no longer conform the patterns of our thinking to our own corruptible, selfish, insatiable, unstable, fallible, changeable, limited, earthbound will—but to instead conform to the incorruptible, all-beneficent, unchangeable, life-producing, enlarging, eternal will of God.*

Your will doesn't stop operating your body. If it did, you might as well have your mind and body laid to rest in a bed to expire for lack of anything to do! No, God does not *take over* of people's bodies, but works through a life only as much as He is invited and allowed. Your own will *must* remain in operation of the behavior and responses of your body—*yet in obedience to the higher will of God!* Where once there flowed from our deadened lives a sullied stream of unholy impulses, the born-again mind now functions as a relay point through which the impulses of a holy God are now the primary instigator. His very actions are reproduced through us. It is this new thinking allowed in any individual that will reveal the presence of a new mindset in operation.

> **"My son, give me your heart and let your eyes keep to my ways . . ."**
> **(Proverbs 23:26)**

Your personal will is to come into concert with God's holy will in a CO-OPERATION of your body's behavior and responses. God's will is the new OPERATOR, but your will is a vitally necessary CO-OPERA-TOR with essential duties to perform that are not in the scope of the OPERATOR'S prerogative: duties such as obedience, submission, receptiveness to instruction, the upkeep of nourishment, and the maintenance of proper periods of stillness and quiet rest.

This relationship of OPERATOR and CO-OPERATOR is exactly parallel to the relationship between a RIDER and his trusted STALLION. To accomplish any substantial tasks together as a team, the rider's horse has to *choose* to follow its rider's command, and do so with split-second responsiveness—without hesitation. That takes trust—and trust takes time and the experience of consistency in the relationship between OPERATOR and CO-OPERATOR. But it also takes a breaking of behavior and response patterns solidly established in the horse over years of roaming the prairie as a maverick. Such a break in the pattern of previous usage of the horse's bodily energies can be accomplished only through special training and discipline and the *renewing* of its mind.

Similarly, the only way the old behaviors and responses in certain situations and under certain impulses will *ever* change is by the renewing of our *own* minds. The reason each of us acts as we do is because the thought patterns of our limited and confined minds have been played out again and again over our lifetime, worn into place like the grooves of an old vinyl record.

> **"You were taught, with regard to your former way of life, to put off your old self, which is being corrupted by its deceitful desires; to be made new in the attitude of your minds; and to put on the new self, created to be like God in true righteousness and holiness."**
> **(Ephesians 4:22–24)**

Renewing implies a remaking—an improving—a rebuilding. To accomplish a mind-renewal project, certain things must be brought to mind:

1. There must be a pre-conceived, pre-drawn plan to which the person that's being remade will conform.

2. Any obstructions to completing the process of remaking must be identified and discarded.

3. Only the highest quality material should be incorporated, and that quality must be maintained.

THE PLAN

Changing habitual behavior patterns takes time and consistent effort. It's hard work to go from an unhealthy junk-food-eating couch potato to a health-conscious devotee to personal fitness and well-being. Likewise, it takes an absolutely extraordinary output of time and hard work to move from the lifestyle of the health-conscious devotee to personal fitness, to the strictly disciplined, highly-focused lifestyle of an Olympic level athlete! The most essential step in preparation for any individual's successful makeover is a well-defined plan, compatible with one's own basic design. Ready to fit.

Thanks to God that the pattern we have is the life of Jesus Christ! But on the way to cloaking ourselves in mantle of His perfect righteousness, we must make sure this new outfit is specifically cut to fit us—to highlight those areas that were weak and hidden—to soften features always too bold, too pointed, or too harsh. If you don't wear His righteousness well, it tells.

A complete makeover should never be rushed; go at the pace that will get the job done right. Some makeovers go painstakingly slow, often because what is being made over is weak and shaky and will be damaged in the process if pushed too fast. At other times, it is because what is being made over is resistant, refusing to give in and break down so as to be added upon and improved.

Some makeovers are completed so silently that what has been made to be new and improved is a surprise to any who were aware of the previous condition.

Some makeovers are never completed because of laziness. Sometimes it's because the redesign specifications were inconsistent with the God-given nature of what's being made over. This is somewhat like planning to have the most capable horse on the ranch made over into the new ranch foreman, responsible for supervising the efficient performance of all the hired hands. This is a transformation that is totally out of order with the sphere of a horse's God-given capabilities—and unless such an unnatural transformation is a miraculous requirement for one of God's supernatural plans, pursuing it is nonsense. In the same way, it would be unwise for a 6'-6", 350-pound, thickly muscled, Olympic-level weight lifter to attempt to make himself over into a diminutive 150-pound, agile, flexible Olympic-level gymnast.

Finally, a makeover should never ever be rushed, because the absence of the necessary amounts of hard work for a superior job done will mean a mediocre or poor job done . . . of little value and even less impact. The result will not improve upon the previous condition of what has been made over, and will peel, crack, and crumble away in the briefest passage of time—disintegrating as if there had never been a plan in mind!

To sum up, if you want to see a bucking bronco made over into a trusty stallion, pick a plan that fits the horse. If the horse is strong, plan for it to pull and carry. If the horse is fast, plan for it to run races. If the horse is clever, plan to have it chase down other wild horses. If the horse is intimidating, let it help contain the livestock. If the horse is calm and gentle, use him to train the children how to ride. If the horse is loyal, keep him always as your personal mount. The point is, plan to have the horse do what the horse already does best—and with time and hard work it can become one of the most important in the stable.

When God gets hold of our lives, corrals us into the boundaries of His love, and shows to us an entirely new way of life, He does so to magnify what He has already placed in us, and accomplish with our lives purposes not yet imagined.

No Longer Necessary

One of the healthiest and most liberating things in this world to do is to throw out the garbage. If you have the plans for a renewal project laid out, it's time to clear out the place of the things that no longer serve a purpose—things that are broken—things that are cheap and inferior—things that are a hazard to safety! Space is created when garbage is thrown out, allowing for new and quality materials to be moved in, and allowing maneuvering room for the rebuilding work to proceed unhindered. Space that leaves the area uncluttered and stripped bare of all that was old, deteriorating, and an interference in the building of the new framework for living that has been carefully planned to stand upright and true:

> "Put to death, therefore, whatever belongs to your earthly nature: sexual immorality, impurity, lust, evil desires and greed, which is idolatry . . . You used to walk in these ways, in the life you once lived. But now you must rid yourselves of all such things as these: anger, rage, malice, slander, and filthy language from your lips. Do not lie to each other, since you have taken off your old self with its practices and have put on the new self, which is being renewed in knowledge in the image of its Creator."
>
> (Colossians 3:5, 7–10)

A radical renewal in the way a person lives his or her life demands the disposal of what is no longer necessary. This needs to be done with the same finality as when a butterfly finally breaks free from and shakes loose the hardening shell of its previous caterpillar casing. Why? *Because every former pattern for living is imbedded in that old self*; if the old self is not completely thrown off and instead is repeatedly allowed to reassume its now obsolete position, then it is certain that what once behaved as a caterpillar, once again taking the appearance of a caterpillar, will begin to behave as a caterpillar once more. In order to leave the old behaviors behind, the new ones must be cultivated and cherished in their place!

NEW, TRUE, AND IMPROVED

You are what you eat. What you've physically consumed all your life is all your body has had at its disposal in its effort to become what it is today. That also is true with whatever you've taken into your mind all of your life. When all is measured, your patterns of consumption throughout life have greatly determined whether you are now in a deficient, average, or excellent condition!

Whatever your case, to be renewed means an improvement. Don't bother to complain about the condition of your life. If you can no longer tolerate what you're mind's been feeding on most of your life—if its been low-grade and has left you dysfunctional, or lacking the right "stuff" to enable your contributions to be valuable to others—CHANGE YOUR DIET. Upgrade your consumption to the highest dietary levels. *You can't improve **output** without increasing and then maintaining a higher quality of **input**.* If you want to increase what your wardrobe's putting out, you increase the quality and maintenance of the clothes you put into it. If you want to increase what your lawn's putting out, you increase the quality of the fertilizer and maintenance you put into it. If you want to enhance your body's output (appearance), you increase the quality of your diet and the maintenance (exercise) you put into it.

The same is true of your spirit. Why else, but for the reason of a higher standard of living, do we welcome into our lives the holiness of God's life-giving Spirit and abide therein? The same goes for our minds! TO RENEW OUR MINDS WE MUST FEED INTO OUR MINDS ONLY THE BEST MATERIALS AVAILABLE.

> ". . . whatever is true, whatever is worthy of reverence *and* is honorable *and* seemly, whatever is just, whatever is pure, whatever is lovely *and* lovable, whatever is kind *and* winsome *and* gracious, if there is any virtue *and* excellence, if there is anything worthy of praise, think on *and* weigh *and* take account of these things [fix your minds on them]."
>
> **(Philippians 4:8; The Amplified Bible)**

Put the best in, and you'll see the best emerge. When you consider the disparity between the ideal mental diet and what you and I *actually* allow ourselves to regularly watch and hear and memorize and think upon, there is most likely an urgent need for a change in diet. Restructuring eating habits (even if its your mind doing the eating rather than your mouth) first takes a strict clearly laid out plan. From there it takes careful diligent adherence to the plan. It is a process that cannot be rushed . . . and its up to you to do. If someone else is making the choices you need to make in order to knock aside habits that you yourself act out, then you will not end up changed at all, persons having wasted their time. *YOU* have to make the choice to cooperate with a blueprint for renewal.

Remember that the One *operating* the whole makeover process in you not only drew up that blueprint especially for you, but He's always on site within you as well. God is an on-the-job personality. Your job is to cooperate. Take advantage of His hands-on management, and an extraordinary renewal will take place in your life. Since you have at your call someone whose declared business is to take care of you, go to Him in the way we've been given to do so. PRAYER. In fact, we will discover the habit of prayer to be about the most practical of the furnishings we will ever install into the new layout of our thinking and behavior. It is a direct line to the Architect who redesigns our lives. Having immediate access to someone with such a wealth of experience for up-to-the-minute supervision of your personal process of change is a supreme advantage not to be ignored or underestimated.

Working with the One who custom-designs your whole program for mental renewal, the one we just read outlined in **Philippians 4:8**, is a dream opportunity come true. In the end, you will find yourself conformed, in our own unique way, to the perfect design of God.

Stick to the new regimen! Give time for the new habits to be fed properly and take hold! Put what works the best into consistent practice. **Work the best in—and then watch the best work itself back out!** Remember God's point of view.

If you have a new horse, a maverick you have purchased at a sacrificial price, you will wish it to be of special use to you. Having studied this horse and determined its potential, you will devise a unique plan for bringing out its assets while breaking all the old habits that will prove a liability in its new life of service. You will bring the horse to water regularly, groom and brush him, and feed him the highest quality foods and grains. Run it through its courses over and over again—and then again some more—in the new tasks and responsibilities it must become accustomed to. Soon enough this new horse will become a tried and true COOPERATOR of the highest order, producing great contributions to your overall operations, according to the changes installed by the OPERATOR Who feeds its living!

STOP AND THINK.

To pursue His purposes as my own
is only the beginning of all my potential.

I will surrender to God everything that I was.
I want more.
I want everything I can possibly be.

This is no passive act of compliance;
it is my creative choice of co-operation.

LIVE A LIFE WORTH GIVING.

HIGHWAYS

I climb the sky-rising superhighways . . .
fresh paved conduits of communication
crisscrossing junctures
bridging the summits of Heaven to the terrain of my life.
Conversational roadways between me
and my Father on high
built for two-way travel and transport.

I'm learning to go up every day;
my Father awaits my approaching praise.
My greeting is warm with thanksgiving He's earned
for the good gifts He's sent since last we met
expressed to me
down these highways
of His Word and my prayer between us stretched.

I offer to Him my life again;
That's how our best exchanges always begin.

But if I come angry at Him and the world
accusing unfairness and hardship and pain
His words of compassion calm me . . .
He listens to me;
I don't lose a friend.
If I come confused, His words give me vision
If I'm tired, He carries our whole conversation
If I choke off my words, too embarrassed to face Him
my Father's whispers hush my heart's cry of shame
and He comes visiting me
with new meaning again
down the trade routes of love between us.

Now shipments of holiness are starting to show
arriving aboard promises I've come to know;
supplies of His Word to me
sent to construct
the stature of Christ
in the state of my smallness.

Deliveries to me
are always received
down the same lanes of prayer I've driven to His throne
to place at His feet
my needs.

Chapter 7

Conversational Trade Routes: The End Of Self-Reliance

"In the beginning [before all time] was the Word (Christ), and the Word was with God, and the Word was God Himself. He was present originally with God. All things were made *and* came into existence through Him; and without Him was not even one thing made that has come into being. In Him was Life, and the Life was the Light of men."
(John 1:1–4; The Amplified Bible)

The power of God is in His expressed Word. When darkness had swept into this universe, God said there would be light and it was so. When the ancient Hebrews whom He had delivered out of Egypt were without direction, God commanded that there would be Law and it was so. When His people could not live according to the perfect standards of those commandments, God promised that there would come a Savior, and it was so. That Savior would in fact be the living embodiment of God's creative Word . . . a person with the power to speak miraculous change into effect.

At certain crucial points in my life I have transcribed my conversations with God. I wrote down my questions, my statements, my weaknesses, my fears, and then wrote down the responses He impressed upon me. I've learned that His responses come to pass. I recognize His "voice"— the gentle intent, the correcting tone, and the encouraging quality of

His compassionate words are wholly unmistakable. Here is an excerpt from a journal transcription dated May 11, 1990 of my dialogue with my Lord as I sought His direction for my life, along with my future wife:

Become a writer.
Draw and paint the word of God for it is the world's window to
    eternity.
Use your skills primarily for the writing of books
to broadcast and proclaim my Name and my nature
to young and to old at home and abroad.
Speak when you must . . . Perform when you should
Be bold . . . Be courageous . . . Fear not . . .
I go already before you and prepare for you a way
BRIGHT, COLORFUL, EXCITING
I HAVE EQUIPPED YOU WELL FOR THE BATTLE—
FOR THE FIELD OF LABOR I HAVE GIVEN YOU TO TEND.

The harvest you/two will bring in will be plentiful

> For whom do I write Lord?

For everyone wise and ignorant, full and needy.

> Why?

Because I love them all.

> When?

You have already begun. I will bear the fruit/seeds to their season
of planting and regrowth.

> What seeds?

The ones that have been falling from you for years though you
have not truly seen.

The ones in my folders?

Correct.

I love you Father.

I love you too, Son/son.

One who is born again will look in the mirror and not necessarily see anything different . . . but there is, in fact, something radically different. We can now begin to hear God's words—commands, warnings, and promises as they are spoken to us through the Bible, through impressions in our thought life, through the new perceptions of supernaturally-energized life, through the teaching and preaching of our pastor, or even through the voice of a loving friend. And when God speaks to you, His words always come backed up with the power to change everything. For He is "the God who gives life to the dead and calls things that are not as though they were." (**Romans 4:17**) OUR GOD IS THE ONE WHO CALLS INTO BEING THAT WHICH DOES NOT YET EXIST.

Is it any wonder the psalmist writes, "Let my mournful cry *and* supplication come [near] before You, O Lord . . . deliver me according to your word!" (**Psalm 119:169,170; The Amplified Bible**)? Of Whom else could it be said, "In my anguish I cried to the LORD, and he answered by setting me free." (**Psalm 118:5**)? Who else holds this power— "Incline your ear [submit and consent to the divine will] and come to Me; hear, and your soul will revive . . ." (**Isaiah 55:3; The Amplified Bible**)?

This is the power that flows behind the voice of our God:

"For my thoughts are not your thoughts, neither are your ways My ways, says the Lord. For as the heavens are higher than the earth, so are My ways higher than your ways and My thoughts than your thoughts. For as the rain and snow come down from the heavens, and return not there again, but water the earth and make it bring forth and sprout, that it may give seed to the sower and bread to the eater, so shall My word be that goes forth out of My mouth: it shall

not return to me void [without producing any effect, useless], but it shall accomplish that which I please *and* purpose, and it shall prosper in the thing for which I sent it."

(Isaiah 55:11; The Amplified Bible)

What an awesome thing it is then to receive even the smallest word from the Lord—for it shall surely come to pass! Even more amazing than this is that the Lord desires to have whole conversations with us! "Call to me and I will answer you and tell you great and unsearchable things you do not know" (Jeremiah 33:3), says the LORD. Even more astounding than all this is that God would instruct us to come gather at his feet to receive intimate one-to-one counsel on the facts of our living—in effect, to infuse our static lives with the powerful current of His all-enacting words!

True prayer is far more than mere conversation. It is actually a transaction. It is dynamic. New things occur. A change in the landscape of our living takes place. His all-creating words drop into our lives—like atomic bombs from our own home base cascading from the sky to miraculously pulverize the limitations that hinder us. They come in answer to our S.O.S. to deliver us from the Enemy. Miraculous events explode into being. Released from the dust like mushrooming clouds, our praise and thanksgiving are thrown upward.

A supernatural exchange takes place.

Now, we know that the Almighty Creator has much to offer us. We, after all, have needs. His words carry a cargo of power into our lives in answer to the specific requirements of our needs. This power has no end to it because of the eternal nature of the Truth from which it is drawn—this power works in us in spite of the fact that we have always been weak. This power cleanses because of the purifying nature of the eternal Life from which it is drawn—in spite of the fact that we have always been soiled.

What, then, of any value do we have to offer Him? What good can come from us? Over the centuries, some have offered Him young bulls on an altar. Others have offered a string of good deeds. But the Lord has made it plain that He desires free-will offerings that could not be considered <u>freely</u> offered if He *commanded* it to be and therefore it was so:

> "I will praise the name of God with a song and will magnify Him with thanksgiving, and it will please the Lord better than an ox or a bullock that has horns and hoofs."
>
> (Psalm 69:31; The Amplified Bible)

Prayer is a two-way pipeline. Precious goods freely flow. Power flows from on high. Praise rises up from below. Prayer is operated on a principal so simple that the smallest child in a kindergarten Sunday school class can master it as readily as the wise grandmother who is an elder in the church. Prayer is initiated just as easily by a gentleman learning disabled from birth and unable to grasp the alphabet as by the seminary student pursuing her doctoral degree.

I'm speaking of the principle of call and response. Our call for His help. God's response. His call for our attention. Our response. The great call for a loving relationship. What is your response?

BEST OF FRIENDS

At its best, prayer works as an act of faith between friends. The reason you bother to call is that you rest assured that your friend will respond to your need. Your call is a matter of trust. You call on a friend because you don't have to know the future to know that the love your friend has proven for you will cause him or her to stand by your side again and again. The deeper the love between you and your friend, the deeper the assurance no matter what secrets you express, the response returned will always affirm your best interests. Fear of indifference, condemnation, or backlash finds no room to take root when loving hearts are pressed so near.

Jesus knew this well. His Almighty Father was also His Friend. That's what made it so easy for them to set aside quality time for one another. The Bible emphasizes that "**Jesus often withdrew to lonely places and** prayed." (**Luke 5:16**) The best of friendship, in all its breadth and depth, carries within it extraordinary security.

> "There is no fear in love. But perfect love drives out fear, because fear has to do with punishment . . ."
>
> (1 John 4:18)

Faithless prayer, full of fear that our God is not really paying us any attention—or that He'll outright spite us—is as meaningless an exercise as basing any relationship on cynicism, suspicion, and withdrawal. Roll this thought around in your head: When you first drew near to Jesus Christ, and invited Him into your daily life, you were inviting Him to become your friend. He accepted your invitation—and He befriended you as well. In other words, He, to whom there is no equal, likes you. Yes, *you*. And there's nothing He enjoys more than sharing the day with you. But this is not a friendship of equal footing. It is the friendship between kid and big brother, student and teacher, servant and king, P.O.W. and Liberator. Therefore, he says:

> "My command is this: Love each other as I have loved you. Greater love has no one than this, that one lay down his life for his friends. You are my friends if you do what I command. I no longer call you servants, because a servant does not know his master's business. Instead, I have called you friends, for everything that I learned from my father I have made known to you."
>
> (John 15:12–15)

One thing about a friend is that he or she knows our weaknesses—well enough, as is always the case with close friends, that there is no point trying to keep our skeletons jammed into the closet. As a matter of fact, that's one of the many benefits of a very close friend—they keep us honest enough to face the truth about ourselves. The one person we deceive most in our lives is the one staring back at us from the mirror with guilty eyes. The best friend in our life is the one in whom we will confide about why we did, didn't do, or never did. That is the person who's loved us enough to become an expert on who we are . . . and yet shields us from shame! That is the person who helps us answer the questions we didn't even know were there . . . because the hardest thing to see is ourselves.

We speak of and define love in mysterious terms because it is supernatural; it is the very substance of God, higher than our nature and our ability to entirely understand. We sense, at the very least, that it is the highest aspiration of humankind. We are too small to contain it; it contains us. We are in the midst of love when we enter the presence of God, and *we* are increased.

So now roll *this* thought around in your head: "Jesus loves me." Why? Because He always loves—it is His nature! So extraordinary is His love that He gave up His own life and handed it over to you. And what a life! A wonderful, infinite, too-fine-a-life to be summed up in words. A life that is the sum total of all good things. This is the Word of God, God's Good News: *that a Holy God would offer us His best friendship.*

How then can we give anything less in return than our best friendship to God? To do so we must stay in touch with Him. Prayer is the means we've been given to do so. A growing friendship doesn't survive unless communication is continually revisited. Just think of it: something so simple as drawing near to the Lord in prayer promises us that the presence of the Creator will always be near!

INCREASING ENCOUNTERS

Families and friends (and even pets), through their constant interaction, have a tendency to learn and acquire the habits, qualities, and practices of one another. But in the case of time shared between one who is unlearned and one who is mature—as with a small boy and a father figure—the impressions made upon the least experienced of the two is immense.

In our relationship with God, we are the children. We are the ones with everything to learn, and now that we have been granted eternal life through our association with Jesus Christ, we have time for Him to show us everything there is to learn. When you have *everything* to learn, after one year's time you've learned nothing; in 100 years time, next to nothing. The point is that with all this learning to do, we are going to have to spend lots of time in close contact with our role model. The more we associate with Him, the more His qualities are going to rub off on us kids.

> "Show me your ways, O Lord, teach me your paths; guide me in your truth and teach me, for you are God my Savior, and my hope is in you all day long."
>
> (Psalm 25:45)

When quality time is continually being devoted to seeking an audience in the presence of God, you can expect to be bathed by the glorious characteristics of God: light, growth, procreation, magnification.

LIGHT. The essence of God. The visible, measurable evidence of the Source—for the closer to it one steps, the clearer all things become, the easier it is to move, the quicker the heart beats. The light invigorates. The light is life. The light is energy. The light is power unleashed. Life, energy, and power openly reveal their basis in light. From the imperceptible aura of light and heat generated by and surrounding all living things, to the cold shimmer from the nighttime stars, to the pleasant red glow from a burning log, to their perpetual glare from the flaring sun, to the shocking flash from a bolt of lightning, to the blinding white balloon of a nuclear explosion. Prayer ignites us like living lanterns to carry within us the pure glow of heaven. *Once we have seen the light, we then can be a light.*

> "When Moses came down from Mount Sinai with the two tablets of the Testimony in his hands, he was not aware that his face was radiant because he had spoken to the LORD."
>
> (Exodus 34:29)

GROWTH. The activity of God. A living body is an organism having organs with specialized functions. A living organism extends itself— just as the Body of Christ extends itself. This is called growth. Anything of God is eternally alive. Anything that is always alive will always grow! Any individual who becomes one with Christ becomes an organ in His

Body's growth. An organism's growth occurs from the inside, pushing outward. Prayer creates an avenue inviting more and more of God's growing presence into us. The force of His life is irresistible. If we allow Him place to grow within us, then our personal growth will *match the rate of growth* He's established for the whole of His Body, His Church, His Creation.

PROCREATION. The motivation of God. Paul said this to the faithful brothers at Colosse:

> "All over the world this gospel is producing fruit and growing, just as it has been doing among you since the day you heard it and understood God's grace in all its truth . . . For this reason, since the day we heard about you, we have not stopped praying for you . . . in order that you may live a life worthy of the Lord and may please him in every way: bearing fruit in every good work, growing in the knowledge of God, being strengthened with all power . . ."
> (Colossians 1: 6–11)

As does any good father, God responds when his children have needs. That includes our need to be a help to others in need. When we pray one for another, we set ourselves in the gap between our presence in the Light of God and another person's hour of darkness. Standing in that gap, we offer ourselves as spiritual lenses to focus the intensity of the Light on the need we are beseeching our Father to meet. And God's grace—His unmerited favor—is transmitted into the life of the person we are praying for; not necessarily because the person being prayed for is deserving, but because God responds to the call of His "Heart." We invite a rush of God's grace as we pray. Then we funnel that flood into a powerful stream to hit a specific target by our specific prayer for a specific need in a specific life! And when that light strikes the darkness, new hope springs up in the afterglow!

MAGNIFICATION. The effect of God. Because God has absolutely no equal—because above all others He reigns supreme, His rarity, His importance, and His value are incomparable. His Name is magnificent. Most excellent. Praiseworthy. It would therefore seem to be some miraculous act of grace—some incomprehensible gift of Providence that we who are His people are "called by [His] name"! **(2 Chronicles 7:14)** It is like the chip of worthless stone that is chosen as the setting for the largest, most flawless, most perfectly cut diamond eyes ever have seen. The value of the diamond is undiminished—the chip of stone, however, is magnified by its permanent attachment to a radiant beauty; the light of the diamond forever adorns it. And what is our attachment to this great God who reigns above us? A simple connection: *We humble ourselves and we pray.*

THE PRESENCE OF POWER

To punctuate any discussion of prayer one must talk about raw power. Not power as the world measures, but immeasurable power as God alone possesses. Power that our God has chosen to make available to His children, His representatives in a hostile land, His ambassadors, His agents.

> **"The priests and Levites stood to bless the people and God heard them, for the prayer reached heaven, his holy dwelling place."**
> **(2 Chronicles 30:27)**

Satan is named by the Word of God as "the ruler of the kingdom of the air" **(Ephesians 2:2)**. But although his dominion and his demonic agents canopy over the entirety of the Earth as a cloak of darkness, prayer *rips* through that cloak like a bullet, faster than the speed of an onrushing thought when launched toward God's throne by those who call Him Master.

There's an undercover operation underway. God slipped into the death march of human affairs in the form of a man named Jesus Christ—and an explosion of His Light took place like the supernova of a star in cold space. Underneath the cover of the musty blanket of sin that still shadows the Earth from recognizing God's Son, points of light are continuing to erupt. Lives are aflame with the truth of God's grace.

His mercy has been made visible in us. Men, women, and children are continuing to invite His holy presence to burn pure within them.

His presence incinerates our daily pollutions—burns on the fuel of His endless compassion—and generates the power of unconditional love. It's the burning of this endless resource that creates the points of Light. Through prayer, we've become windows—the access points for Heavenly Light to infiltrate a rebellious Night.

As agents then of Jesus Christ's Light, we have importance to the plans of God. When Jesus prayed, sending up requests to the heavens to prove the power of God to a faithless people, God immediately responded with moves of power. Power was rushed down from Heaven to Earth according to the specific word of Christ—Who spoke only as His Father desired. Things were changed for the better—all in a demonstration of the nearness of mercy. God is committed to making His mercy known. Now that we've been given a share Christ's agenda (and a measure of His faith in our Father), when *we* pray in His name, GOD MOVES WITH NO LESS POWER FOR OUR NEEDS THAN HE DID FOR THE NEEDS OF THE MAN CHRIST!

The key word is **WE**. No agent of the Lord Jesus Christ can be very effective operating independently. We are uniquely called to operate as <u>inter</u>dependent components of a holy orchestration. Today as we pray, if our prayers are effective, it is because we pray in agreement with Jesus' leading; He is conductor now of our daily events. It is His made-up mind that determines what we pray for. And when **WE**, as assemblies and fellowships and congregations, unify our prayers and raise them in concert, it is Jesus' promise that the chorus of our requests will generate a power to raise the mountaintops! Showers of blessings will come pouring in.

> ". . . I tell you that if two of you on earth agree about anything you ask for, it will be done for you by my Father in heaven. For where two or three come together in my name, there I am with them."
>
> (Matthew 18:19,20)

STOP AND THINK.

I will impact someone's life today.
I'll relay an unexpected gift.
I will pray for a need that is not my own;
my lips will carry another's name into the presence of God.

By prayer:

I will destroy the power of men against me
by becoming a friend that they do not yet know

By prayer:

My family and friends will be saved
as God changes their lives by speaking their names.

LIVE A LIFE WORTH GIVING.

SUBMISSION

It takes all you've got to give up all.
The large possessions and the small.
Those things kept hidden shelved up high
that satisfy
too short a time;
those lusts in the closet well out of view
those things that "feel so good" to do
those drives and passions pushing you
to do things you don't want to do
but still you very much want to do
but still
you feel so bad when through.
Nothing good is accomplished,
nothing gained.
You inflict yourself
like you always do
with self-pity
guilt
and
shame . . .

but

what it takes is giving in
your closetful of secret sins
given to God as the very things
that come between you and Him
so Christ can enter broom in hand
and throw out the trash again

and what it takes is trusting Him
giving Him charge of housekeeping within
to inspect your life daily with corrective direction

filling all rooms with Godly intentions
sweeping the shelves of secret lusts.

But what it takes is giving up.

Chapter 8

And A Little Child Shall Lead Them: The End Of Self-Indulgence

"He called a little child and had him stand among them. And he said: 'I tell you the truth, unless you change and become like little children, you will never enter the kingdom of Heaven. Therefore, whoever humbles himself like this child is the greatest in the kingdom of heaven.'"

(A quote from Jesus in Matthew 18:2–4)

One of the greatest blessings I've ever received has been the opportunity to teach elementary-age children at Hunter College Elementary School in New York. I found myself the recipient of many gifts and offerings. Because I taught art classes and displayed many of my artistic inclinations to the children, certain of those children deemed it appropriate to every so often place in my hand *very* original works of their own. To keep. Made just for me. They would walk up to me and say, "This is for you." I would thank them, and they would skip away to play. The children were serving what they perceived to be my needs. From their point of view, what better way to show their art teacher they care than by giving him gifts of what he considers important.

The word **humility** is derived from Latin roots meaning "low" . . . "earth" . . . and "on the ground." And that's the place where all children live. All children are quite familiar with the fact that they live life at a very low eye level. In fact, in order to reach anything of great altitude in this life, they depend on someone much bigger than they are either to lift them up from ground level, or to bring that which they desire more within their reach.

This is also the place where humility begins. That's why children so readily obey. That parent figure who by opening a child's doors, giving a child rewards, and showing the inexperienced child what and how to go about doing *proves* that he/she is worthy to be listened to. That's why children so immediately return love—when someone big and busy stops and bends to the earth just to greet them, smiling such large smiles, saying such sweet things, sweeping them straight to the sky for a hug, love is eagerly returned.

Strange how so many of us adults have been deceived into thinking that humility is attained by walking around, eyes down, face scraping across the ground, crying, "Oh! Oh, woe! Oh, woe is me!" That's not humility—that's degradation and self-abuse. No. Humility isn't something we manufacture within—it's an external matter of fact. **Humility demands not that I debase myself, but simply that I turn my eyes upward and notice how very much greater Someone else is than me.**

Jesus knew that men and women are taught that as "adults" they no longer have to look up to anyone. But Jesus did not consider Himself a "grown-up"—He considered Himself the Father's first-born Son and remained as humble as any other child. Now that Jesus is high and lifted up, we are commanded to remember our earthbound point of view. **He commanded that we make ourselves think as children again by returning again to a child's point of view.** We would be stubborn not to do so—but of course, stubborn is exactly what most of us are! And that's dangerous. A loss of the proper perspective, a loss of humility is the beginning of stubbornness, and stubbornness is the beginning of disobedience. And disobedience is the end of love for God.

SELFISH RESISTANCE

If you, like I, confess publicly and sincerely that Jesus Christ is your LORD and Savior and the One Whom you love most of all, then you, like I have a decision to make today. The choice is whether or not to truly *yield* to the lordship we claim He has over our lives! Unfortunately, most of us neglect making this choice until it's too late to do anything but cry and repent over the tragic, unnecessary mess-ups produced through our unyielding heart! I speak of a choice that is our sole responsibility to originate and act upon. God does not twist His children's arms, nor does He manipulate us against our wills like marionettes on strings.

A personal choice is called for that, if made daily, will once-and-for-all end our stop-start, halt-go, year-in, year-out, one-step-forward, two-steps-backward, tear-stained melodrama of interrupted growth, retarded spiritual maturity, and ineffective service! Such a pattern of stunted living, I know from experience, is unbearably draining and entirely self-induced. Such living is the result of our unwillingness to, without reservation, make the choice that Christ instructed us to make in all His loving authority:

> ". . . If a person [really] loves Me, he will keep My word [obey My teaching]; and My Father will love him, and We will come to him and make Our home in (abode, special dwelling place) with him."
> (John 14:23; The Amplified Bible)

When Jesus spoke these words, He was in the midst of an intimate conversation with men who were the closest of His disciples—men who publicly and proudly professed their love for Him. But, as usual, Jesus cut right to the heart of the issue by implying that just because someone <u>says</u> they love a person, doesn't mean the receiver feels loved at all! Jesus knew, for example, that if a person's deepest needs cry out to be held and cuddled, then it doesn't matter if you're the greatest listener, give gifts on all occasions, and are always available when called. Unless you shower that person with hugs, he or she will rightfully tell you,

"You don't really love me." For true love always fills the ache of another's needs. So Jesus Christ, God in the flesh, put it all in a perspective we could surely understand:

> **"If you [really] love Me, you will keep (obey) My commands."**
> **(John 14:15; The Amplified Bible)**

Simply because we are habit-forming creatures, the choices we make we will make again and again. **We have heard the cry of God's heart.** His deepest desire is for us to freely obey Him as our *sole* Commander-in-Chief. Which leaves us with a choice. It is the choice between loving God well, with freely offered, wholehearted OBEDIENCE—or showing Him a clench-fisted, resistant mockery of love, with a heart shut up tight by the barricades of STUBBORNNESS!

> **"See how each of you is following the stubbornness of his evil heart instead of obeying me."**
> **(Jeremiah 16:12)**

To carry *any* attitude other than humility . . . to willfully choose to do other than what we are directed to do by One too great to ever be unworthy of our obedience . . . is an awfully stubborn stance to take. Examine a definition of the word stubborn, paraphrased from Webster's dictionary text.

> *STUBBORN: Obstinate (Keeping firmly to one's opinion or to one's chosen course of action . . . not easily persuaded to turn from one's course); Not easy to control or deal with (does not easily allow another to intercede in, take action about, or be the solution to a problem); A defiant stiff-necked demonstration of one's own self-imposed authority in a situation by purposely ignoring, discounting, or obscuring the voice of the justifiable and proven authority . . . or by unjustifiably elevating one's own voice above others who are equals.*

It's a terrible reality that even if most of us will acknowledge our patterns of stubbornness with the other humans we relate to daily, we do not think to test ourselves for the very same stubbornness exhibited toward God! This self evaluation is urgent if our intention is to be a "cooperator" with God—because the ultimate outcome of a careless, undedicated, and stubborn attitude will always be this: REBELLION. Rebellion against God has a primary and secondary route, but both routes lead to the bottomless pit of Hell. Let me explain.

The primary route is *the choice to willfully disobey.* It was just such a choice by a certain being that earned him the title Satan . . . translated, "the Adversary of God." But rebellion also has a secondary route, which is *the abdication of any choosing whatsoever as to whether or not one is going to obey the commands of our Most High God.*

How dangerously we live! We forget that anything useless to the good work of God is going to attract His Adversary like a fly to untended meat. Before we realize it, we will find our lives infested with the maggots of indifference and self-indulgence. Therefore, the same results are produced by **stubborn resistance to obedience** to the commands of God, as by **willful disobedience** of the very same commands: Satan ends up standing with his foot on top of our necks and having his way with our lives.

What a hindrance to the work of God to have those who claim to be followers of Christ lying uselessly and shamefully about with the Adversary trampling unimpeded upon their lives! And not because these hostile forces have any particular power to have their way with a child of God's life—but because followers who opt not to obey open their lives to become a breeding ground of idle living and unapplied potential that the angelic Rebels of God find quite comfortable to hang around with.

Have we forgotten that Christ is "the head of the body, the church" (**Colossians 1:18**) . . . that the church is made up of those worldwide who acknowledge that Jesus Christ has saved them (**Ephesians 5:23**) . . . and that we who have accepted Christ as our Savior have therefore become His living Body stretched across the face of the Earth? That places us in a position of high responsibility—**and makes it necessary that we remain highly responsive to instruction**—in order to function properly as Christ's hands, feet, limbs, and vital organs operating for Him in this world.

But if members of the "Body" stubbornly resist what the "Head" is telling them to do, the resulting dysfunction will bear a tragic similarity to the many diseases of human physiology and neurology which impair or destroy our motor responses. All the vitality and power that would normally be channeled through us is aborted. Such breakdowns and failures within us, the Body of Christ, are the result of wavering somewhere between blessed obedience and useless rebellion. No wonder there is both anger and pleading in Christ's voice, as John reveals this prophetic message to the members of the church in ancient Laodicea:

> "I know your deeds, that you are neither cold nor hot. I wish you were either one or the other! So, because you are lukewarm—neither hot nor cold—I am about to spit you out of my mouth."
>
> (Revelation 3:15–16)

We human beings must be the most wishy-washy, non-committal, fence-straddling, self-sabotaging creatures that ever existed. The angels were decisive enough to either choose complete service to God or outright warfare. We, on the other hand, like to excuse ourselves from responsibility. Perhaps we feel that God must certainly understand our natural reservations about giving Him our all. Perhaps we are convinced that He understands our timidity as we shuffle along the borders of the work field and watch others faithfully serve Him—pouring out their blood, sweat, and tears—carrying out tasks that, to us, seem far above and beyond the call of duty. Perhaps we feel positive that God understands our prudence as we stand aside and project the possible outcomes of committing to a life of unhesitating obedience. Perhaps we feel it *is* asking a bit much to hand over *total* authority to this God fellow to Whom we sing love songs every Sunday morning.

Well, He certainly *does* understand us . . . all too well. Our track record of decision making and the blood it cost to redeem what we had lost couldn't be clearer to Him. It is our fumbled handling of our first responsibility—to superintend over the life of this planet He'd entrusted to us—that became our first irresponsibility and that leaves us without any excuses.

> "He who is not with Me [siding and believing with Me] is against Me, and he who does not gather with Me [engage in My interest], scatters."
>
> (Luke 11:23, The Amplified Bible)

These are Jesus Christ's words, and we know that His primary purpose is to save those His Father sent Him to save. Precious lives. Ripe and ready to be gathered up and find their places in God's new land. The most insufferable result of our stubbornness is that our resistance to participating in our Savior's continuing work—especially now that we enjoy the benefit of having *ourselves* been saved by that work—is tantamount to negligent manslaughter. Yes, the same people whom Jesus Christ has intended to save . . . people close at hand . . . are losing their grip on life itself while we ineffectively twiddle our thumbs!

Our resistance to the discipline of humility and obedience can make us useless to God—and any agent of God rendered useless to God is a boon to the Adversary whose great desire is to see God's glory scattered to the wind. God's glory can be found in the praises of His Creation. But by our puttering about on the fringes of a harvest field visibly short of laborers (**Matthew 9:37**), we allow countless souls within our reach to go untouched by God's mercy . . . and those who go untouched will never know to praise Him. Instead of being gathered up, these souls will wither quickly as the season for harvest passes them by.

Moreover, our inactivity becomes a stumbling block to the true laborers in the field who lose time and energy climbing over our idle bodies to get to work. They are overloaded by being left to do their fair share of God's work *plus* ours. They are subtly convinced that if others stand by idly, then the tasks at hand must not be as urgent as God has said. What a disservice to God!

Finally, consider this. If you have not yet chosen to place all that you own, all that you are, and all that you are going to become, smack in the middle of God's camp and entirely subordinate to the spoken word of Christ's daily command—then you have allied yourself with the plan of His Adversary. Before you were even aware of his schemes, the Adversary's plan was to make your living in vain. God is an *abundant-opportunity* employer, and anyone choosing unemployment in God's camp is not a part of God's camp—becoming easy plunder for Satan who prowls like a lion on the borders of the camp. Idle wanderers into the outer territory of the Enemy are unreliable laborers to God. And unreliable laborers can threaten the integrity of even the best-intended work.

"One who is slack in his work, is brother to one who destroys."
(Proverbs 18:9)

THE GREATEST COMMAND

Although the discipline of any kind of service must be humility and obedience, the only motivation must be love. Other motivations such as sense of duty, self-respect, the expectations of others—are each dependent on too many other factors and will falter and fail us at times. But true love . . . undying love . . . resurrected love . . . is all by itself an unfailing motivator. Perfect love is God's own original motivating factor and will propel us into service for the sake of even those who show us only hostility . . . just as it did Him for our sake.

It isn't truly love if it isn't willingly, generously, unreservedly acted out. Nor is it love unless acting it out costs us something dearly. Love will make us vulnerable and touchable. It will expose us to burdens we cannot carry alone and introduce us to the victories won only by exploits in the art of loyalty. Love will mean the death of independent pursuits. When true love is manifested, there is one sure result: individuals yoked together in the joy of unbreakable fellowship.

The fact is, God Himself commands us to truly love. That is, **He commands us to choose to benefit others according to their needs and as a gift, not as a favor to be earned—not from our leftovers, but at our sacrificial expense.** When asked which was the most important commandment, Jesus replied:

"Love the Lord your God with all your heart and with all your soul and with all your mind and with all your strength. The second is this: Love your neighbor as yourself."
(Mark 12: 30, 31)

But how can anyone command us to love? The answer is that only God could . . . for "God is love" (1 John 4:16). It's okay for love to command us. It does all the time. And aren't we always at our best when we allow the call of love to direct us?

That's why our children are the best of us. That's why it's such a tragedy that children born in the late 20th and early 21st centuries are becoming "adults" before their time.

Children truly love. Have you ever had a little child smile and charge toward you to fling their arms about you and squeeze you with such utter abandon and reckless strength that you're almost bowled over? You can't help but squeeze back. That's love as it was commanded to be. Within the little child is the blueprint for love.

THE PLAN OF LOVE IS ALWAYS TO INITIATE CONTACT. It is the little child asking us with generous affection, "Can I stretch my hands out and hug you and make you feel warm like my pillow?" Love's plan is to draw near to another heart . . . just as Son of God drew near to you. Love turns a stranger into someone you call your own friend.

THE PROCESS OF LOVE IS ALWAYS SACRIFICIAL. It is the little child asking us with genuine intention, "This is important to me, so can I share it with you?" Love's process is to walk with an attitude communicating to another that what is mine is freely offered . . . just as the Son of God gave freely to you. Love will give up some property to make the common ground of fellowship between yourself and someone you call your neighbor.

THE PRODUCT OF LOVE IS ALWAYS GOOD PLEASURE. It is the little child asking us with cheerful expectation, "Can I please you more?" Love's product is the fulfillment in satisfying another's needs . . . just as the Son of God finds good pleasure to instill in you His joy. Love's pursuit will always be the happiness of someone you call your own.

THE PURPOSE OF LOVE IS ALWAYS INCREASED LIVING. It is the little child asking us with innocent calculation, "Can we *stay* friends?" Love's purpose is to maintain all that's gained when yourself and another form a relationship . . . just as the Son of God promises to do when He forms a relationship with you. Love's purpose is to continuously increase the bond of fellowship with those whom we call our own.

We are commanded to love. Tender loving care is the most necessary thing of all, making it also the greatest driving force of all. People daily give their lives for the sake of what they find necessary. But only true love is necessary. Only true love can save our planet from death, granting instead the promise of resurrected life. Of course, true love is only found at the Source of what is True; WHEN WE ARE COMMANDED TO LOVE WE ARE ACTUALLY COMMANDED TO DRAW NEARER TO OUR GOD. And that's just what it takes to live a life worth giving. For God knows that the greatest sacrifices are all offered in humble obedience to the command of the greater necessity.

GREAT AND SMALL

There are people whose names are envied throughout the world because of their wealth and notoriety. The rich and famous. The stars of stage and screen. The great athletes. The leaders of government. The corporate tycoons. And there are people, past and present, whose life stories are so remarkable that their names have been incorporated into folklore, history, and legend. **But many of us will never know the names of the greatest men and women to have walked the face of this Earth.**

They sacrificed notoriety. They sacrificed standing above the crowd. They sacrificed all the stature that adulthood supposedly brings. They lowered themselves to become the little children of God once again. The Almighty became their Daddy in Heaven. Even as they answered the call of our God, we must know it is our calling as well:

- To cry out our neediness to our Heavenly Daddy as honestly as does any child.
- To receive our Holy Daddy's love and attention as hungrily as does a child.
- To leap into our Great Daddy's arms . . . relaxing . . . feeling safe, and thankful as a child.
- To look up to and talk about our Almighty Daddy as adoringly and confidently as a child.

- To believe that what our Daddy says is true as totally as does a child.

- To submit to our Daddy's authority and rule as unquestioningly as does any little child.

- To obey our Daddy's wisdom and perfect instruction as faithfully as does a child.

- To seek out the fascinating little truths about life that only the eyes of a child bother to see.

- To communicate as boldly, honestly, and fearlessly as do the mouths of babes.

- To hear, listen to, and internalize what's new as quickly as do the ears of a child.

- To remain as open and available to teaching and discovery as does the mind of any child.

- To be as unconditional with our love, as free in our sharing, as un-prejudiced in our interactions, and as inviting to new friends as does Jesus, the most excellent big brother!

"Let the little children come to me, and do not hinder them, for the kingdom of God belongs to such as these."

(Luke 18:16)

THE UNLOCKED TREASURE: GIVING

You and I have been given much. Our Almighty Father, out of a parental love, is committed to providing for our necessities and beyond. Unknown to many, He has established what I might call "The First Law of Guaranteed Returns"—a law which has been a source of provision in interdependent relationships since the genesis of creation. The network of gravitational pushings and pullings that keeps our solar system of heavenly bodies all in orbital relationship with one another—the fine balance of give-and-take between animal species that causes the chain of life in biological ecosystems to thrive—these are large-scale examples of the truth of a particular law which Jesus illuminated:

"Give, and it will be given to you. A good measure, pressed down, shaken together and running over, will be poured into your lap. For with the measure you use, it will be measured to you."

(Luke 6:38)

Children operate through the principles of this law as instinctively as they hold their breath under water, or cry out for food when they're hungry, or throw out their arms and knees when they fall. They initiate this law when they reach out to us so that we may reach out in turn and lift them to our bosom. They initiate this law when they say to another child, "I'll be your friend if you'll be mine," or "I'll trade you two of my cookies for your lollipop."

But there is another law that is based on this same principle of reciprocity. It, too, has been set in place for our provision. But if perverted in its application, it also holds the power to devastate any life unyielding to the will of God. I will call this "The Second Law of Guaranteed Returns," and the Bible outlines it thusly:

"Do not be deceived: God cannot be mocked. A man reaps what he sows. The one who sows to please his sinful nature, from that nature will reap destruction; the one who sows to please the Spirit, from the Spirit will reap eternal life. Let us not become weary in doing good, for at the proper time we will reap a harvest if we do not give up."

(Galatians 6:7–9)

Little are these two Laws used in tandem; *if they were, remarkable provision for our needs and desires would simply begin to show forth.*

If you're looking for love, resolve to carry out the little love you have within you to fill up vacancies in other lives, and you will reap an immeasurable harvest of that very same love returned, multiplied many times over, to you!

If your heart is hardened with long-standing resentments, you need only apply yourself to soften the callousness of another's stony heart, and the ability to forgive those who trespassed against you will swell unexpectedly from your *own* heart's storehouses!

If you suffer joylessness, just commit to help others dismantle the embattlements that imprison their emotions, and *YOUR* walls will tumble as well!

If you lack peace, sow peace into the hearts of all you are acquainted with and, as the laborer quenching the raging fires of useless quarreling, feel free to reap for yourself a replenishing supply to cool your own lips!

If you need healing, administer all the first aid you can manage to the wounds of those within your reach. The healing you ministered will be ministered back to you with such care and compassion that not even the *scars* from your own wounds will remain!

And if you haven't found it within you to forgive yourself for being who you are . . . for the damage you believe you've caused . . . for the lost years you can never reclaim on your own, then plant this message of the grace and mercy of God into ears wherever you may go—and God Himself will deliver a return far outweighing the value of all the lost dreams you could never attain on your own! You will have no choice but to consume the bounty of His forgiveness and His favor given without reservation . . . yes, to one even such as you.

STOP AND THINK.

The final estimation of the worth of my life
will ultimately be calculated
not on the basis of what I've accumulated
but on how much of my substance
has been unconditionally offered,
presented
to God and man alike
as a timely response to the call of love.

LIVE A LIFE WORTH GIVING.

Part 3.

"DO NOT BE OVERCOME BY EVIL, BUT
OVERCOME EVIL WITH GOOD."

THE NEW DIET

Feed my mouth with your Love, Lord
your food will sustain me
your words will give rise to new strength on their own
I now empty myself
of what nearly has killed me
the impurities that fed me I press from my bowels

the lies so acidic they caused me to retch
the bitterness long gnawed that had broken my teeth
the self-seeking that soured my love & affections
the waste of my time stopping up my production
the anger that burned on my tongue
and the ignorant slop to which I was accustomed

I've dined insufficiently on the sin of this earth
Now I turn over my plate and I shut up my mouth
My first appetites once had entire control
of the intake that had constipated my soul
but I hunger no more for the poisons I ate
My food is to do Your will today

Lord, now that my life is a service to You
I've no time for the food of rebellion against You
And I fast for my cleansing
my interior need
to be freed
from the aftertaste disobedience leaves

Lord, I've got a new craving
I desire a diet both simple and sweet, yet life-giving, too
My appetite now is for high-content dining
So I've decided to empty myself
of my Self
and instead be filled with You.

Chapter 9

Infilled By The Highest Living Being

"But in a great house there are not only vessels of gold and silver, but also [utensils] of wood and earthenware, and some for honorable *and* noble [use] and some for menial *and* ignoble [use]. So whoever cleanses himself [from what is ignoble *and* unclean, who separates himself from contact with contaminating and corrupting influences] will [then himself] be a vessel set apart *and* useful for honorable *and* noble purposes, consecrated *and* profitable to the Master, fit *and* ready for any good work."

(2 Timothy 2:20, 21; The Amplified Bible)

I used to be a bit mixed up about what makes a person important. In my teens I developed an obsession with being considered other people's "best friend." I wanted to be the most important person in other people's lives! I had no idea the need I was most concerned with was my own. Having been a loner since childhood had left a massive void for human companionship which I tried to fill in the quickest way possible while a young adult: singling myself out as candidate for "The Most Important Person" to the very few friends I had.

What I was too naive to understand was that importance is not arrived at by *self-appointment*—it is an answer to an *invitation* to be what another person needs. Instead, I was imposing myself, blanketing others with acts I felt sure would be considered above and beyond the call of duty of a mere rank-and-file friend. Suffocating acts. I was *always* around doing nice things for my friends. I was doing things I wasn't even asked to do.

But doing does not always equal giving. In fact, it was years before I could see that few people were more needy than I was. Anyone who could see through me would have known I had nothing inside me to offer; I was void and desperate for self-worth. I was looking to be filled with my friends' affirmations of my importance to them. But to be important, you have to be filled with something to give. Years of not relating to people left me vacant of the stuff people need.

Those who are the most important of all—those who are the most useful of all—are those who have the greatest capacity to measure up to filling the needs at hand around them. The Latin root of the word *capability* defines it as the full measure of whatever it is a person or thing can take in or take on.

It is our willing obedience to be applied toward the insufficiencies of our comrades in the human condition that will determine our potential as individuals to be esteemed by God as important. The fact that we each have measurable capacities is why the apostle Paul, in **2 Timothy 2:20,21**, explains that from God's point of view we all have the potential to be vessels with the capacity and usability for significant purposes. Fortunately, once persons are born again and living as a sacrifice, holy and acceptable to God, their capacity—with no human effort involved—will supernaturally grow and stretch. The simple ingredient of importance will always remain this—**TO BE FOUND FILLED WITH ONLY THAT WHICH IS NEEDFUL.** A parable will illustrate.

Before a balloon is truly a balloon, it is a limp shapeless piece of rubber with no definition, filled with nothing at all. It serves no purpose this way, and is simply a thing with great possibility, temporarily empty of what will fill it, give it definition, and help it to take the shape it was designed to take. When balloons are filled, some become round, some become long and thin, some take the shape of giant caterpillars, some sprout giant black mouse ears. Some balloons have the capacity to carry a man across an ocean. Some balloons take a shape so intricate and spectacular they fly in a Macy's Thanksgiving Day Parade.

The greatest balloons of all are the ones with the most empty space to fill! But before a balloon can become all it can be, it must be filled with a formless, expanding gas. The gas breathes life into the limp, shapeless, purposeless balloon. The rubber or fabric swells and stretches, giving definition to a heretofore hidden shape. A balloon designed to be round will not turn out instead long and thin, or sprout Mickey Mouse ears on its dome. To do so would distress the boundaries of the balloon and destroy it with a loud pop. The gas flows in with ease, and as the volume of the balloon is inflated to conform itself to the infilling flow, it becomes more distinct and unique and identifiable and ready to serve its purpose.

The infilling of the balloon makes it more than it was previously. Having taken shape, it becomes desirable and precious to those who celebrate, to those who love, to those who are simple, to those who are free, and to those who enjoy colorful floating objects. Only the balloon that is filled ever rises. As it is with the balloon, so it is with the man or woman filled to capacity with the Spirit of God.

Because Jesus lived on Earth as a human being, even He had to first receive the infilling of the Holy Spirit from Heaven before our Father put Him to use. *He was filled to overflowing with God's Spirit!* The first chapter of the Gospel of Mark records Jesus' simultaneous baptism in water and baptism in the Holy Spirit. Baptism is a one-time event. The word baptism is derived from a root that means *to dip*. Water baptism, first administered by John the Baptizer, is a symbol of being "dipped" into a new dispensation by God—where an individual is plunged beneath the waters to succumb once-and-for-all to the "death" wrought by wickedness. Individuals are lifted up again to "new life" by no effort of their own, but by the mercy and grace of a compassionate Savior, and by their yielding to His hands extended.

Jesus, a Jew by birth, was baptized in water. Like all others who came to yield themselves into the strong arms of John the Baptizer, He was "resurrected" to a lifestyle far superseding everything culture and family alone limited Him to be.

As Jesus was being baptized, the Bible says He and other witnesses saw Heaven open and the Holy Spirit descending upon Him . . . like a dove (**Mark 1:10**)! And what better manifestation than a dove! At the beginning of the Old Testament when Noah and his family (the only ones righteous left among humankind) drifted above the flood in an ark of safety, it was a dove that came to him carrying the promise of life to a lost humanity (**Genesis 8:6–11**)! Out of Noah would spring a new generation of humanity. And at the beginning of the New Testament, when it was the life of Christ (the only one perfectly righteous living among humankind) that would become an ark of safety to lift us above a flood of sin . . . there too came a dove, this time carrying the promise of a new and supernatural life to a humanity still lost! *But out of Jesus will spring an eternal generation of humanity.*

So Jesus, a mere man by birth, was also baptized in the Holy Spirit. Like all others who come to yield themselves into the strong arms of God, He was "resurrected" to a lifestyle far superseding everything humanity alone limited Him to be.

Sweet Holy Spirit. The rich, manifested presence of God was the Living Water overflowing in Christ's life to spill over and drench the multitudes crowded about him with supernatural refreshing in the heat of the Mediterranean afternoons. And always they clamored for a little more of the power that always seemed to fill Jesus. How did Jesus stay full?

When the neediness of the pressing multitude drained Him, we know He often went off by Himself to pray. When He returned, He was always full of the sweet Spirit of God again. But there was something else that Jesus did.

It's true that in order to be a vessel for good in this world we must be filled to capacity with that which is good—for Jesus said these words to us: "**Why do you call me good? No one is good—except God alone**" (**Mark 10:18**). But we human beings already are filled with lots of stuff. Whether we like it or not, we collect in our spirits the sediment and contaminants of our daily existence in a polluted world. Jesus, knowing this fact of life yet desiring to live His life filled to capacity, undertook on the day of His baptism a regular practice we would do well to imitate. He was compelled to clear out extra space for God. He emptied Himself. Jesus fasted.

EMPTYING THE VESSEL

"If anyone would come after me, he must deny himself and take up
his cross and follow me."

(Mark 9:34)

Fasting is not easy. It is physically draining. It is emptying. That, in
fact, is its importance. We know that our very flesh has been so corrupted by indwelling sin that it doesn't live and grow forever as God
originally designed. Instead, it weakens and dies. When you think about
it, the first cry of the flesh after exiting the womb is the desperate cry for
food. It is our original craving and our first indulgence. We don't just
need it—we demand it. We'll even steal to get it.

In Jesus' day, crucifixion upon a cross was a terrible method of ex-
ecution established by Roman authority. His command that His followers take up their crosses and follow Him is far more than a prophetic
insight that He was destined to die on a cross. It is His forthright pro-
nouncement that anyone who would follow His example by living their
lives as a sacrifice must, like Him, from time to time deny certain forms
of sustenance. Certain things must be put to death. Not just any kind of
death. The slow, punishing, openly visible process of crucifixion.

What in us deserves this kind of death? *That which is already under
penalty of death.* That which remains so infected by sin it is condemned
to return to the dust from which it came (**Genesis 3:17–19**). That which
was captured and exploited in the Devil's attempted murder of humanity: *the flesh.*

"But I discern in my bodily members [in the sensitive appetites and
wills of the flesh] a different law (rule of action) at war against the
law of my mind (my reason) and making me a prisoner to the law of
sin that dwells in my bodily organs . . ."

(Romans 7:23; The Amplified Bible)

We were born with Adam and Eve's priorities. Adam and Eve first
sinned by making it a priority to satisfy their craving, to fill their stomachs with what God told them never to eat. Therefore, what better place

to start denying ourselves than with the original craving that sent us toward the grave?

Once again, we were born with Adam and Eve's priorities.

The bodily organ that we call our stomach is specifically designed to consume only food. It exists for no other reason. Anything we ingest that is not good for food upsets it. Nourishment is its reason for being. And the stomach must have food in order to function; otherwise, it ends up empty, shrunken, and functionless.

The stomach is part of God's design for our fulfillment. How many things are as physically satisfying as the feeling of the filling of our bellies? In order to feel full, there had to be an organ in our bodies that gets filled up. Hence, the stomach—intended purely for our physical satisfaction.

But Jesus had a new set of priorities. He began a forty-day fast on the day that He was baptized. He stopped filling His stomach for a period of time. And the Devil came to trick Jesus into filling Himself with loaves of bread for His self-satisfaction.

> **Jesus answered, "It is written: 'Man does not live on bread alone, but on every word that comes from the mouth of God.'"**
> **(Matthew 4:4)**

Jesus knew that satisfying ourselves physically doesn't keep our bodies from weakening and eventually dying. Jesus also knew that our physical bodies are temporary housings—and necessarily so. With God we have the promise of eternal life, far from feasible with a body that may last at the most 100 years or so. The real reason the Devil could not tempt Jesus to fill His belly was because Jesus' gaze was fixed on the resurrected life ahead . . . with a body subject neither to physical constraints nor demands. A spiritual body, not a physical one (**1 Corinthians 15:42–44**). He already had begun to wean Himself on the kind of food that was spiritual; not the kind meant to fill merely the stomach, but the kind that can satisfy the innermost man. Jesus knew best of all that a full stomach gets empty again, but a spirit fulfilled lasts an eternity! The

Bible confirms that God will indeed do away with the stomach, and food for the stomach (**1 Corinthians 7:13**). Jesus was born with new priorities.

When our spirit is born-again, our specific design to consume the presence of God is restored. Our spirit exists for no other reason. Anything we ingest that is not of God is upsetting to His Holy Spirit within us. God is our reason for being. Our spirits must have God's presence in order to function; otherwise our spirits end up empty, shrunken, and functionless.

God has flip-flopped the hierarchy of our natures. The structure we were born with is one wherein the dominant operations of our being are carnal, and spiritual operations are suppressed.

FLESH - consciousness of the five senses; physically-dependent
SOUL - consciousness of identity/emotions; socially-dependent
SPIRIT - consciousness of the spirit realm; God-dependent

Being born again establishes a new hierarchy wherein the dominant operations of our being are spiritual, and carnal operations are suppressed.

SPIRIT - consciousness of the spirit realm; god-dependent
SOUL - consciousness of identity/emotions; socially dependent
FLESH - consciousness of the five senses; physically dependent

While the flesh is still with us, if we feed it first, it grows weightier than it should ever be. An imbalance occurs that quickly begins to bury our awareness of the presence of God—under dust and clay it seems. Jesus took no such chances. He didn't starve Himself . . . He just regularly denied His *flesh* by fasting, by feeding first on the presence of God.

There is much about fasting we should strive to understand. Fasting is not just a matter of regularly denying the flesh and crucifying the power of its cravings to ever again dominate our lives. It is also about drawing spiritual sustenance by tapping into the veins of God's life-sustaining spirit. As goes God, so go we. As He would now do, so should we. That's why Jesus could say with honesty to His disciples, "**My food is to do the will of him who sent me and to finish his work**" (John 4:34). His heartbeat found its rhythm and its strength to the beat of the compassionate heart of God!

So though fasting requires periods of severing the supply of anything that feeds the sensual cravings of our own flesh, if during that time we can be an aid to someone suffering needless deprivation, we will find food in giving as God would give. During a fast . . .

- the sensual gratification of tasting food and flavors is denied; instead we find our food in providing food for the hungry.
- the sensual gratification of tempting aromas and fragrances is avoided; instead our noses are tickled by the fresh smell of the newborn we lovingly cradle on our shoulder.
- the sensual gratification of passionate touching and heated sexuality is denied; instead we find tactile satisfaction in giving a long hug and a soft caress to someone who is in pain, or a tender kiss for our spouse.
- the sensual gratification of loud music and human chatter is denied; instead we find refreshment for our ears by the sound of our own voices shouting out in worship, whispering songs of praise toward heaven, reading a story to put the kids to sleep.
- the sensual gratification of the overwhelming amounts of visual-media entertainments is denied; instead we will find a feast for our roaming eyes in the genuineness of the tears and the smiles on faces of the lost led home to Christ.

Yes, fasting empties us of ourselves that we might be filled to capacity with the Spirit of God. But it is the Spirit of a kind and merciful God Who has swung low to offer life and love without reservation to all who are near. He reminds us never to forget:

"**Is not this the kind of fasting I have chosen: to loose the chains of injustice and untie the cords of the yoke, to set the oppressed free and break every yoke? Is it not to share your food with the hungry and to provide the poor wanderer with shelter—when you see the** naked, to clothe him, and not to turn away from your own flesh and blood?"

(Isaiah 58:6, 7)

GIFTS FULFILLED

Different balloons, when filled, do different jobs. Some balloons are perfect at a birthday party for inciting a light and playful atmosphere. Some are perfect for recording the weather. Some balloons are perfect for leisurely travel. Some are perfect for spectacular parades. But, just the same, all balloons must be filled with an expanding gas.

> "There are different kinds of gifts, but the same Spirit. There are different kinds of service, but the same Lord. There are different kinds of working, but the same God works all of them in all men."
> (1 Corinthians 12:4–6)

Born-again individuals all over the world together make up quite a complex organism of people with different vocations and abilities all called to one cause—to sacrifice their lives in co-operation with the One who has shared out to each a portion of His eternal life. The Bible says, "Now you are the body of Christ, and each one of you is a part of it" (1 Corinthians 12:27). Like the parts of a physical body share the same blood flow, we in Christ share the same Holy Spirit.

At the moment we asked Jesus to come save our lives we were baptized or "dipped" into the holy presence of God, and Jesus washed us clean of our sin in the purity of His righteousness. That baptism in God's Holy Spirit was a one-time only event, part of Jesus' provision for those He calls His own. Though Christ would physically ascend and depart from us into Heaven after His resurrection to take His rightful place beside His Father, Jesus *also* promised that He would never leave His followers without His guiding presence in their midst. So Jesus Christ made a way to remain the central presence in the earthbound lives of every one of us who know Him as Lord. His followers were told to expect:

"... the Holy Spirit, Whom the Father will send in My name [in My place, to represent Me and act on My behalf] . . ."
(John 14:26; The Amplified Bible)

And that Holy Spirit remains in us as long as we remain partakers of the holy presence of God. After all, we are what we eat.

So the question we are getting to is not, "Do I have the Holy Spirit?" All who have enthroned Jesus Christ as the Lord of the kingdom of their heart also share His attendant Holy Spirit. The important question now is, "*Do I intend to keep myself filled to capacity with the Spirit?*" The well being of our place in the Body of Christ depends on the vitality of the flow within us. How? Consider the huge body of a cartoon character's balloon that floats in a Macy's Thanksgiving Day parade. If any part of the body of the huge balloon is deflated of its capacity, it dangles limply and conspicuously from the lofty body—shrunken, functionless, and empty. As the deflation of a part of the balloon can throw the movement of the entire balloon off balance, so it is with the man or woman insufficiently filled with the Spirit of God.

"Now to each one the manifestation of the Spirit is given for the common good."
(1 Corinthians 12:7)

"Just as each of us has one body with many members, and these members do not all have the same function, so in Christ we who are many form one body, and each member belongs to all the others. We have different gifts, according to the grace given us."
(Romans 12:4, 5)

Each member of a body is a gift to all the others. Different parts of the body have different natures because they are purposed for different functions. Often we waste time feeling sorry for ourselves, guilty because we don't possess someone else's giftings.

For instance, some may lament that they don't possess another fellow's unrelenting hunger to take in and digest the Word of God . . . never considering that only *some* are gifted to be digesters of the Word for the

Body's intake. A few specific parts of the human body function as the digestive system; the rest of the body is expected to reap the benefits of being freely fed. Others lament that they're financially unable to circulate the basic necessities of life to needy members of the Body . . . never considering that only *some* are gifted to be the system of circulation for the Body's vital needs. A few specific parts of the human body function as the circulatory system; the rest of the body is expected to reap the benefits of being freely supplied.

The following is an excerpt from the *World Book Encyclopedia* on the subject of the human body. In its description of the systems of the human body it says that the **"body is made up of several systems of organs. Each system has its own special job, but all the systems work together to keep the body alive and functioning properly. The major systems of the human body include: (1) the skeletal-muscular system, (2) the digestive system, (3) the urinary system, (4) the respiratory system, (5) the circulatory system, (6) the nervous system, (7) the reproductive system."**

Likewise, the Holy Spirit's purpose is to keep the Body of Christ alive and functioning. Each one of us who seeks to be filled with the Spirit will find ourselves expanding in a *certain* area of function. He uses us in His service to the Body because we make ourselves available to be filled. We must be aware of the significance of what we are becoming and why. Filled up and expanding, our lives are God's gifts to make the whole Body well balanced.

The skeletal-muscular system provides the strength, framework, and locomotive force of the body. Such are they who bring the gift of active, supportive, and practical SERVICE to others in the Body of Christ. And the message of God to the one who is filled and purposed to expand in this capacity: **"If it is serving, let him serve . . ."** (**Romans 12:7**).

The digestive system of the human body "prepares food so the cells can use it, absorbs the food into the body, and eliminates any material that cannot be absorbed" (*World Book Encyclopedia*). Such are they who bring the gift of biblically accurate, well-studied, balanced TEACHING to others in the Body of Christ. And the message of God to the one who is filled and purposed to expand in this capacity: ". . . **if it is teaching, let him teach . . .**" (Romans 12:7).

The urinary system purifies the flow of blood by sifting and separating that which is harmful or useless and excreting it from the body. Such are they who bring the gift of a infiltrating, corrective, and clarifying PERCEPTION to others in the Body of Christ. And the message of God to the one who is filled and purposed to expand in this capacity: "**If a man's gift is prophesying (perceiving), let him use it in proportion to his faith**" (Romans 12:6).

The respiratory system floods our blood with an oxygen-rich fuel so necessary that if the system is impeded for a only a matter of minutes, the body collapses, the brain is damaged, and the whole organism quickly dies. Such are they who bring the gift of renewing, invigorating, revitalizing ENCOURAGEMENT to others in the Body of Christ. And the message of God to the one who is filled and purposed to expand in this capacity: ". . . **if it is encouragement, let him encourage . . .**" (Romans 12:8).

The circulatory system is the body's method of internal transport—delivering and depositing oxygen, food, and redistributing materials to designated locations throughout the body. Such are they who bring the gift of timely, regular, consistent GIVING to others in the Body of Christ. And the message of God to the one who is filled and purposed to expand in this capacity: ". . . **if it is contributing to the needs of others, let him give generously . . .**" (Romans 12:8).

The nervous system initiates, regulates, and manages the efficient activity of all the systems of the body. Such are they who bring the gift of steady, responsive, functional LEADERSHIP and ADMINISTRATION to others in the Body of Christ. And the message of God to the one who is filled and purposed to expand in this capacity: ". . . **if it is leadership, let him govern diligently . . .**" (Romans 12:8).

The reproduction system of the body is equipped to conceive life and support that life in the quiet safety best supplied by the body. Only when that life is fully developed and can survive the rigors of the surrounding world, the body gives birth to that life. Such are they who bring the gift of an all-encompassing, carefully protective, nurturing, maternal COMPASSION especially to those newly conceived or those weak and vulnerable within the Body of Christ. And the message of God to the one who is filled and purposed to expand in this capacity: ". . . if it is showing mercy (compassion), let him do it cheerfully" (Romans 12:8).

> "Each one should use whatever gift he has received to serve others, faithfully administering God's grace in its various forms."
>
> (1 Peter 4:10)

FRUITS OF THE SPIRIT

Some "balloons" are good to eat. Fruits slowly balloon at the ends of branches until they reach a point of ripeness when they are swollen with the best a thriving plant has to offer. When a fruit has reached its fullness, the branch loosens its grip so the fruit may be easily plucked, gathered, and eaten.

> "I am the vine; you are the branches. If a man remains in me and I in him, he will bear much fruit; apart from me you can do nothing."
>
> (John 15:5)

The word fruit comes from the Latin word *frui*, which means "to enjoy." Fruits are that part of a flowering plant which contains the seeds which are its means of reproducing the uniqueness of its kind—especially in a sweet pulp that is usually edible. These seed-bearing structures grow for the purpose of being separated and scattered from their place of origin in the hope that new life unique to its kind might be able to take root and bear fruit elsewhere. Because of our connection to Christ, ever-filling us with the vitality of His Spirit, just like any other thriving branch we too begin to show forth fruit. *This fruit will bear the seeds of life unique to the kind that Jesus Christ lived when He walked upon the earth.*

". . . the fruit of the Spirit is love, joy, peace, patience, kindness, goodness, faithfulness, gentleness, and self-control."

(Galatians 5:22)

Because of His Holy Spirit deposited in our beings, there has grown within us seeds of the Jesus Christ kind. We are branches of Christ, and like Him—if we remain connected to Him—we will cast to earth the fruit of the Spirit wherever we go.

This sweet fruit attracts eaters; wherever Jesus' fruit grows, when it ripens, it will always attract the multitudes. No wonder. The fact that the word fruit finds its root in a word meaning *to enjoy*, confirms what we all have experienced—*the satisfying nature of God's supply*. To hear the sound of your own teeth entering a fruit ripe with vivid color as cool juice trickles down your cheeks, with the smell of tartness tickling your nose as sweet pulp slips over your tongue—our senses are thrilled! Our bellies say yes. Yes! Spiritual fruit affects us no less, but it is food not to the stomach but instead to the *spirit* of a man or woman:

To bite into the "love fruit" is to find that one bite is never enough . . . for the love fruit holds within it the rejuvenating powers of restoration. The love fruit initiates internal healing. The love fruit causes wounds to knit and reconstruct. The love fruit, eaten regularly, will extend the life of a man such as I. As when my wife, Me'Shae, invested her life into me.

The "joy fruit," when bitten, bursts with a sweet and abundant juice. But the juice is not sticky and syrupy—it flows as freely as water. It refreshes immediately, uplifts low blood counts, and replenishes the strength of the Body's members. As when I allowed myself to laugh with the children I one taught as they each discovered their senses of humor, concocting their first jokes.

The "peace fruit" soothes the pain or turmoil of a bodily system upset or aching. It calms the nerves. Its effects remain active and its flavor abides long after the last bite of fruit was taken. It counteracts the bitter aftereffects of things ingested that should have been left uneaten. The peace fruit is a supernatural antidote to all internal distress. As when I find a moment silent of all voices along the soft waters of a wooded retreat.

The "patience fruit" is a laxative for when our bowels are seized with blockages and extraneous matter that slows the natural processes. The fruit is sometimes sweet and sometimes sour but it always offers unexpected and much needed relief. As when I trod on toward the prize of full redemption, shedding my persistent failings, not giving up on promises of God to totally save me.

The "kindness fruit" is always soft and fills the belly, a special treat served warm. It is a fruit that lightens the weight of a heavy meal just eaten. Once bitten, a fragrance is released that attracts other eaters to the fruit's location. As when my former supervisor and friend Patricia Lambert, a beloved and veteran elementary school teacher and principal, pursues with diligence her work on behalf of children, parents, and new teachers alike—adding to the numbers of those who call her their mentor.

The "goodness fruit" is a fertile fruit carrying within it many seeds. Large and voluminous, it is a meal unto itself. When its seeds take root, many-tendriled vines spring up and radiate outward, spreading flowers and fruit throughout the vicinity. As when my church, The Brooklyn Tabernacle, sends out to an adjacent and needy community a newly ordained pastor and a portion of its faithful membership to raise up a new sister church.

The "faithfulness fruit" is a robust and tenacious variety of fruit able to take root and thrive in the harshest climates. It boosts the Body's protective immune system and has a property that heightens the senses and actually magnifies the ability to perceive the shape of things to come. As when my senior pastor Jim Cymbala, and his wife Carol, director of The Brooklyn Tabernacle Choir, committed themselves to tough it out in the heart of Brooklyn, New York, based on their vision of a congregation dedicated to multiracial fellowship and worship and prayer, and making a "joyful noise" to God!

The "gentleness fruit" has a delicate velvety skin that is soothing to the touch. Its juices are a natural softening lotion for even the most dry and calloused skin. As when men of God—many of whom still bear the tattoos of their youth as the scars of a life without God—lay hands upon and pray for one another, hugging and weeping out of love for their brethren.

The "self-control fruit" is a chewy, fibrous fruit that aids the Body in its regularity. This fruit also serves as a supernatural supplement that aids all Bodily systems in the proper exercise of their function. As when I bond with a trusted brother as an accountability partner, so as to guard my heart against the sin that so easily entangles.

All of these fruits attract eaters. Those that taste find in this fruit a small taste of Christlikeness. By being edible and delightful, these fruits are sure to multiply. As new lives in Christ take root, the life of Christ will be spread among men and women. And all of this comes **only** by remaining filled with the Spirit like a branch remains filled by its sap. As fruit grows unrelentingly in its season, without a murmur of effort on the part of any branch, so it shall be with all who are intimately attached to Jesus Christ. Our fruit will spring from His nature.

"You did not choose me, but I chose you to go and bear fruit—fruit that will last . . ."

(John 15:16)

STOP AND THINK.

After spending a lifetime just full of myself,
it is to my advantage to be filled with Someone greater.

LIVE A LIFE WORTH GIVING.

THE INVISIBLE WAR

We charge Hell's gates
its hinges crack
we push through with our one advantage . . .

it is our Captain who leads the attack!

I'm on the front lines of this confrontation
My mission, to follow my Captain to glory
I'm wounded each day in the Life-or-Death contest . . .

but my Captain brings aid, preserves and restores me.

He was mortally struck by our Foe
He has risen alive to His feet
My Captain takes position at the point of our assault . . .

His upraised shield defends us from the Enemy's fiery darts.

I am just a holy warrior
I have just begun to fight
My blood will pour out in this field if it must . . .

yet I will stand by my Captain in the fury of His might.

This Liberator has come among us
to retrieve every captive who has cried out His name
still within the Enemy's perilous dungeons

out of which, by my Captain's hand, I've been saved!

It is not in the Body armor we share
nor in the weapons of Reconciliation I bear
but in my Captain I have placed my trust . . .

His command has assured us our conquest!

Chapter 10

Inducted Into The Highest Military Assignment

"For our struggle is not against flesh and blood, but against the rulers, against the authorities, against the powers of this dark world, and against the spiritual forces of evil in the heavenly realms."

(Ephesians 6:12)

Sometimes you feel like you're in a fight. Things happen. The worst kinds of stuff comes right down on your head so fast you can't get yourself out of the line of fire. Sometimes it seems you get messed up for no good reason at all. Sometimes it's because you've been messing with what you should have been avoiding. In either case, when everything assaults you all at once, so that you feel like you can hardly come up for air and like you're gonna die in the darkness underneath it all, that's called adversity. And although we scream, "WHY ME?"—guess what— *it happens to everybody*.

Adversity is no accident. There's someone who really wants to give us a hard time. Our enemy is the Devil. He opposes everything that might turn out good; he is called the Adversary of God. Adversary . . . adversity . . . get the picture? When adversity sneaks up and clonks you in the back of the head, please remember as you climb back to your feet that it's your enemy, the unholy Adversary, who's just put a hurtin' on you.

During my first years in grade school, it seemed very clear who my enemy was. His name was James Wolfe—quite appropriately, considering his predatory behavior. I suppose he sensed weakness in me—some flaw that made me easy prey. The fact that I was so distant from the teachers and the other kids made it easy for him to stalk and torment me. Who would notice my being hurt?

I tried to avoid James, but he was in all my classes. He would hit me, poke me, pick at me, push me, laugh at me, insult me, leave thumbtacks on my chair, and all-around bully me. I honestly didn't know what to do about it. At that point in life, I remember knowing what persecution felt like, but I didn't hold enough of any kind of emotion to work up a response—an angry one, least of all. I had limited my give-and-take with people; I had no experience with putting up a fight.

So James had his way with me for a long time before the day came in second or third grade when my anger was ignited. It was during library period, and Mrs. White was supervising. I was sitting alone, reading in a corner of the library, when James Wolfe made his approach. I don't remember what triggered me. A push? A pinch? But my reaction was such a shock to my self-contained mind-set, the incident is recalled only in flashes of memory.

I leaped from my seat to attack James. He curled into a ball beneath me, both his hands covering his head. Both my hands pounded down on his back in a rhythm that punctuated each syllable of my demand that he, "LEAVE-ME-A-LONE! LEAVE-ME-A-LONE!"

I was still beating James when I remembered there were other people in the library. I looked up to see that all my classmates had moved out of their seats to assemble at Mrs. White's desk in the middle of the room; there they became spectators. No one said a word—not even Mrs. White who stood with them. But I could read her eyes under the bangs of her short black hair. More vividly than anything else, I remember how her eyes smiled back at me to give her unspoken approval. She made no move to stop me. So I focused again on what I was doing and pounded James a few more times before my explosion burned itself out.

I received no warnings, reprimands, or penalties for my action that day. Neither Mrs. White nor any other teacher ever commented on it to me. None of my classmates treated me any differently. James avoided me . . . for a while. I realized that for reasons that may have been identical to mine, everybody must have thought it was a good idea for James Wolfe to get beat up.

I was wrong to retaliate against James. James Wolfe was not my enemy—he was like me, a flesh-and-blood little boy. He needed an infusion of love to change the shape of his life just as much as I did. I wonder what would have happened if I had wielded the power to ask James Wolfe to be my friend. I don't remember him having any friends that I knew of in school.

When you strike out for a cause that will right a wrong—when you strike out to end a persecution, even your own—who can argue your fight? But make your shot count by fighting the one who initiated the harm that so angers you. Unless you directly challenge the source of unrighteousness, even as Jesus Christ did, you will never see a day free of conflict, for we dwell in the enemy territory of an unrighteous humanity controlled by the Evil One.

> **"He who does what is sinful is of the devil, because the devil has been sinning from the beginning. The reason the Son of God appeared was to destroy the devil's work."**
>
> **(1 John 3:8)**

We live in a day where God is providing unmerited favor to the unrighteous man or woman who seeks His help. His answer is to offer unconditional love. Likewise, we live in a world where we are surrounded by people who need that help as desperately as we do. God reaches out by filling us with His love and sending us out to touch them. AS THE RECIPIENTS OF GOD'S LOVE, ONE THING WE MUST NEVER DO IS ATTACK THE FLESH-AND-BLOOD PERSONS WHOM, ALONG WITH US, OUR GOD HAS EXTENDED HIMSELF TO SAVE. Though men have opposed God in open hostility, God has not treated humankind as an enemy nor even as its sins have deserved (**Psalm 103:8–10**). God has named His enemy: <u>Satan</u>. This Devil has also been exposed through God's Word as the most devious enemy we'll ever face:

"The thief comes only in order to steal and kill and destroy."

(John 10:10)

". . . that enemy of yours, the devil, roams around like a lion roaring [in fierce hunger], seeking someone to seize upon *and* devour."

(1 Peter 5:8; The Amplified Bible)

Satan came against Christ; Christ defeated him by choosing to lose His life in utter humility upon a cross . . . in spite of Satan's temptations to get Him to choose a more self-important course. Now Christ comes against Satan. As followers of Christ, His enemy is our enemy. Satan is the one we fight. Satan is the only being we have a right to get violent with. And we fight this fight on Christ's terms, with only the weapons Christ chose to use, aimed only at those evil forces (visible and invisible) Christ has targeted for destruction. We are no threat to our Enemy—not even a nuisance—unless we fight Christ's fight, Christ's way, for Christ's purposes alone.

"For though we walk (live) in the flesh, we are not carrying on our warfare according to the flesh *and* using mere human weapons. For the weapons of our warfare are not physical [weapons of flesh and blood], but they are mighty before God for the overthrow *and* destruction of strongholds, [inasmuch as we] refute arguments *and* theories *and* reasonings and every proud *and* lofty thing that sets itself up against the [true] knowledge of God; and we lead every thought *and* purpose away captive into the obedience of Christ . . ."

(2 Corinthians 10:3–5; The Amplified Bible)

IN HIS MAJESTY'S SERVICE

Ask any enlisted man or woman in any branch of service—Coast Guard, Army, Air Force, Navy, Marines—and they will tell you that their transformation into a good and well-trained soldier required enduring many hardships. Military basic training is designed to be severe so as to recondition a man to survive, thrive, and conquer despite the shock of the combat zone. The combat zone is unmerciful in its assaults. It is a place where we must stand our ground against the swell of unexpected and concentrated attacks: where the survival of those who march with us relies on our unhesitating response to command and our action as part of a unit; where our resources are scarce, and manpower spread thinly; where our weapons must be kept under around-the-clock guard; where our safety and our preservation are voluntarily placed at risk; where what we face ahead is always obscured with the unknown.

There is a spiritual basic training provided for all those who enlist as followers of Jesus Christ. Be well aware—our conscription as His soldiers is a part of His call to follow Him. Jesus considered the fight important enough to die for. As is common to heroes, His sacrifice has made His name immortal. But so great was His particular sacrifice, He rose *bodily* to immortality as well! When we first approached Jesus in all our need, we stood before Him willing to die—so that we might be born-again into a Christ-like life. Thus, we were baptized into His heroism; He fashioned a few good men and women. Now that He's made us to be like Him, He must use us as He Himself was used. As His new creations, we have meaning to the world only within the context of God's new design for us:

> **"For whatever is born of God is victorious over the world; and this is the victory that conquers the world . . . our faith."**
> **(1 John 5:4; The Amplified Bible)**

We must be thoroughly disciplined and prepared before we can be of any use in His service. The lives of men, women, and children will be liberated or lost depending on our commitment to battle-readiness. To the timid, this prospect may seem too great a burden to carry. But soldiers throughout history *have* shouldered such weight with great enthusiasm—when it has been accompanied by a great and unfailing trust in the power that has sends one out to fight. Nations call it patriotism. God calls it faith.

If we believe in the Savior Who has set us free from captivity, we will follow Him into the darkest camps of the human spirit to rescue others still in bondage, waiting to die.

If we believe in the beauty of citizenship in Heaven, and in the right of the people of God's Kingdom to assemble here far from home as we, for now, must continue to do, we will take up all the weapons that Heaven provides that we may fight back the invasion of unrighteousness among us.

If we believe in our way of life as exemplified by the life of our own Christ, then we will gladly submit to our own discipline and correction, always ready to answer a spiritual "call to arms," and obedient to our Central Command—that we may be worthy of the title "Defender of the Faith."

If we believe in the fitness of Jesus as our Commander-in-Chief, then we will forsake all other preoccupations and endeavors that we may serve him well.

"Endure hardship with us like a good soldier of Christ Jesus. No one serving as a soldier gets involved in civilian affairs—he wants to please his commanding officer."

(2 Timothy 2:3, 4)

DECLARATION OF WAR

Sometimes an enemy advances so savagely, so indifferent to the value of life, we are left no avenue of response but to clash head-on, knowing only one shall emerge triumphant. The people of God, the recipients of heavenly mercy, are under attack by an enemy of the human spirit who hates the God we now stand for. People who have yet to know God's mercy are held in a fatal chokehold.

When the lives of those you love are being led to the slaughter, declare your resistance and fight this battle well. Your enemy must be made to know you've the will to endure, and a love that won't be surrendered. Your enemy must be rocked with the fear that you are subject to God alone and that your strength is in the God of unlimited supply.

Submit yourselves, then, to God. Resist the devil, and he will flee from you.

(James 4:7)

Your enemy, the devil, is committed to the destruction of all who stand in opposition to his unholy ends. There are two ways by which he rids himself of opponents: He may attempt an assassination, knocking out his target in a quick burst of sniper fire—or he may attempt a seduction, slowly turning his target into the sway of his command. But before he can do any harm at all, before he can even get near you, he must first isolate you. His goal is to sever you from your company and set up the ambush of his choosing.

I once found myself isolated from my company of fellow believers several years ago, as I allowed the increasing time demands of my undergraduate education to become an excuse for steadily decreasing my church attendance.

I left myself open and vulnerable to be drawn into what became one of the most traumatic experiences of my life. I embarked on a naively conceived, long-distance relationship with a girl whom I met on her visit to New York from her home in Jamaica. We were seriously conversing about the possibility of marriage within the ridiculous span of three days . . . it was three months later before I actually asked her to marry me! *It was the worst mistake of my entire life.* This was a mistake that cost my integrity as well as tremendous amounts of money in phone bills, gifts, and plane fare. But I was so committed, so faithful . . . so ill-thinking, so short of good counsel . . . that I was even ready to uproot myself and make a new home in Jamaica in order to make the relationship work. She called to inform me to cancel the flight I had booked for the following week—not to bother to make any more trips—that she didn't love me or want to marry me any more—that I should forget that I ever knew her. I was devastated. I was wrecked.

My platonic friendship with her younger sister eventually bore me the information never communicated to me—that for at least *three months* prior to that terrible phone call my ex-fiancée had been carrying on a relationship with another man in Jamaica. I fell hard . . . emotionally, spiritually, psychologically, even physically. Harder than I had ever fallen before. I can only praise God that He saw fit to lift me to my feet again. I wish I knew then what I know now.

Face it. God invested everything He had available to turn our lives around and lift us to our feet as His soldiers. Which means that life now carries a weight it could never before have supported, God has given us a job and equipped us to do it. We each have an assignment that our compatriots are depending on us to fulfill. So if the Devil can eliminate us, he causes disruption in the march across the battlefield that you, the rest of the believers who make up our attachment, and I, have been ordered defend.

If you fall, the Devil punches a hole in the front lines of your force's mounting faith. He creates a breach through which he can infiltrate, divide, and outmaneuver the advance of your coming ranks. If I fall, someone else must be called by God to take over my assignment. During that delay, another wartime atrocity may be committed—another human life stolen by the Devil.

This is all to say that if you're a follower of Jesus Christ, you're important enough to be targeted by His enemy. So follow your Captain's instructions.

God has provided a place in the rank-and-file in which to encompass you. Therefore, you cannot be singled out and assassinated unless you forget your place in line. *No one is called to stand out; our call is to stand unified in collective strength.* To try and stand head and shoulders above the rest is to get your head shot off. Stay humble; stay low.

"Pride goes before destruction, a haughty spirit before a fall."
(Proverbs 16:18)

You cannot be singled out—seduced to collaborate with your enemy—unless you allow your enemy close enough to listen to his lies. Lies that once gripped your attention. The familiar lies—self- importance, self-reliance, self-indulgence—are still attractive. They are sent to distract you and divert you from completing the assignment directly at hand, and to compromise the cause for which Christ sacrificed His life. They are extended to you because they *are* familiar. What harm is there to reach out for them once again? But beware. They are booby-traps; they will incinerate the purity of your born-again spirit. They are mines; they will tear the legs off your walk with God. They are live grenades tossed at your heart; they will engulf you in a fireball of sin. Do not be deceived. Never move out on your own impulses. Wait for your command. Guard your heart.

> "For if, after they have escaped the pollutions of the world through [the full, personal] knowledge of our Lord and Savior Jesus Christ, they again become entangled in them and are overcome, their last condition is worse [for them] than the first . . . There has befallen them the thing spoken of in the true proverb, The dog turns back to his own vomit, and, The sow is washed only to wallow again in the mire."
>
> (2 Peter 2:20, 22)

TACTICAL MANEUVERS

What is in Satan's arsenal of weapons against us? What is his strategy against the foot soldiers of the Kingdom of God?

HIS WEAPONS ARE ALL FORMS OF FALSEHOOD—PRETENSES, LIES, AND DECEIT. These weapons undermine the Truth that is the underlying stability of our footing. In the midst of our campaign against the darkness, the ground beneath us gives way. We are swallowed in confusion.

HIS STRATEGY IS TO BREAK OFF OUR ATTACHMENT TO GOD'S UNCHANGING POINT OF VIEW SO THAT THE MOMENTUM OF GOD'S PEOPLE INTO ENEMY-OCCUPIED STRONGHOLDS BREAKS DOWN. IT BECOMES "EVERY MAN FOR HIMSELF," AND WE STAGGER AWAY FROM OUR GOAL IN FEAR.

Satan's onslaught is consistent; he uses his weapons with precision. There is no mistaking a battlefield where this enemy has been encountered: it is littered with the souls of comrades paralyzed by confusion. Most of the rest have had their insides torn out by fear and anxiety; and those who've got caught up in a blastfire of renewed sin have been twisted and disfigured beyond any recognition of holiness. All movement has been halted.

Yes, the devil is unleashing his arsenal with increasing bursts of ferocity. Yes, he is holding onto his deepest entrenchments with a desperate finality. But this is because, in spite of the casualties strewn before us, Satan is at the last of his firepower and our ranks are piercing through!

> "[God] disarmed the principalities and powers that were ranged against us . . . triumphing over them by the cross."
> (Colossians 2:15; The Amplified Bible)

It's only a matter of time now. Nazi Germany knew the end was near; the Devil knows it, too. Those who follow their orders without reservation, those who avoid the collapse into falsehood, those who keep their eyes fixed on the prize before them, those march doggedly at the heels of the Savior who leads them, those who attack the chains of captives dying to be free, those wounded but never slowed by the enemy's fire, those never diverted, those offering their lives—they will bring glory to our Commander-in-Chief and wear His eternal *Medal of Honor*.

> "Let your eyes look straight ahead, fix your gaze directly before you. Make level paths for your feet and take only ways that are firm. Do not swerve to the right or the left; keep your foot from evil."
> (Proverbs 4:25–27)

A MIGHTY FORTRESS IS OUR GOD, A BULWARK NEVER FAILING

There is a refuge from the battle. It is the place where the soldiers of Christ stand at ease. It is in the fortress of rest provided for our replenishment and security. This is the place where we gather together—for there, the mighty presence of God sets up camp (**Matthew 18:20**).

God is the strong tower that shields us from the fight; in His presence there is rest from the warfare. Our wounds are attended to; our bellies are filled once again. We can be calm. Our God himself is the holy Citadel whose walls are impenetrable, whose heights cannot be scaled, never by any foe besieged.

Only in the fortress are we prepared again for battle. Only in the fortress do we receive new commands. Only from the fortress do we charge out in obedience behind the flag and spearhead of our exalted Savior. The presence of God entirely equips us:

> "It is God who arms me with strength and makes my way perfect He makes my feet like the feet of a deer; he enables me to stand on the heights. He trains my hands for battle; my arms can bend a bow of bronze. You give me your shield of victory, and your right hand sustains me; you stoop down to make me great. You broaden the path beneath me, so that my ankles do not turn."
>
> (Psalm 19:32–36)

HALLELUJAH! Our Savior goes out before us and our great God has got our backs. We each wear across our chest a banner of light, a beacon fit to penetrate a landscape cloaked in a pall of unholiness. But even as we pierce the darkness ahead of us, a flare always lights the sky above us. They are launched from our mighty fortress by God Himself, illuminations of His holiness, hovering above our path. He never deserts the assembly of His people, even as together we enter the conflict.

If we march in the shoulder-to-shoulder formation that magnifies our strength, supporting each other as we go, shown the way by the blanketing illumination of our God, what dark foe could withstand such light?

In particular, I walk shoulder-to-shoulder with a wonderful woman from Indiana, named Me'Shae. I am married to her. I am able to say that each day for the rest of my life I will choose to love her, shouldering her responsibilities along with my own. Me'Shae is an invaluable treasure to me . . . a gift to me straight from God's heart . . . and a vessel full of His unique love for me. When she acts out her love to me, God pours out Himself through the pores of her flesh. God is the architect of the glowing love constructed between us. He Himself is our shelter overhead, Jesus Christ our foundation. Thus, the home we have together will endure the passage of time, and frustrate the assault of Satan upon our union—and stand.

"The LORD is my light and my salvation—whom shall I fear?
The LORD is the stronghold of my life—of whom shall I be afraid?
(Psalm 27:1)

THE ARMOR WE'VE BEEN GIVEN

Learning how to maneuver in battle carrying the weight of a full suit of body armor and fighting equipment, is part of every soldier's basic training. A warrior without armor will quickly become a needless casualty. No army can afford the easy loss of those trained to be the best they can be. The soldier who disregards his basic equipment in self-defense does not understand the importance of his or her place in the ranks, and stands in contempt of the call to fight the good fight (**2 Timothy 4:7**). Any soldier who aspires to be the best of God's warriors wants to fight to the finish, not be the first casualty. Satan is a serious enemy. Given an opening, he'll stab you in the heart and, without missing a beat, pick up your body to use as a bludgeon to club one of your comrades to death. Defend yourself!

> **"Finally, be strong in the Lord and in his mighty power. Put on the full armor of God so that you can take your stand against the devil's schemes. For our struggle is not against flesh and blood, but against the rulers, against the authorities, against the powers of this dark world and against the spiritual forces of evil in the heavenly realms. Therefore put on the full armor of God, so that when the day of evil comes, you may be able to withstand your ground, and after you have done everything, to stand."**
>
> **(Ephesians 6:10–13)**

Every soldier is equipped before he is sent out to fight. We've been given a complete set of armor. Let's take a quick inventory to make sure all pieces are at hand, clean, and in working condition. Our checklist is in **Ephesians 6:14–17**. It begins:

"Stand firm then, with the belt of truth buckled around your waist . . ."

Have you ever noticed how weightlifters are always careful to tightly buckle around their waist a heavy leather supportive belt? The explosive strength and momentum of the weightlifter, or any other athlete, is generated from their center—the muscle groupings of the abdomen, lower back, hips, and buttocks. The belt of truth girdles, stabilizes, and protects the center of a man or woman—it keeps our new center of balance intact. Truth, tightly buckled, heightens our ability to stand tall and unwavering whatever the task. Truth never gives way. Our posture remains upright. It tightens and focuses the efficiency and strength of our movement, and guards us from crippling injury when struck unexpectedly in battle. To stand in truth is to stand firm and unbowed—and on that belt hang the weapons of our warfare.

". . . with the breastplate of righteousness in place . . ."

Without righteousness as a covering, we are doomed to be carried off the battlefield. If our righteousness is worn carelessly, we present an opening to receive a killing blow; only a miracle of mercy heals a heart cleaved open. The breastplate is designed to protect all vital organs from base of throat to lower abdomen. A soldier pierced in the heart, lungs, stomach, or intestines is helpless on the battlefield. Before we rush out to put a hurt on the enemy, our righteousness had better be fastened over *our* breast.

Be advised: many soldiers have been horrified to see their righteousness slip away in the heat of battle; they took their place in the field unprepared. In their moments of quiet they did not take the time to check and recheck—and if necessary, reinforce—their attachment to their defensive breastplate, their attachment to the Savior, who is called, ". . . **The LORD Our Righteousness**" (Jeremiah 23:6). Fix Him always in front of your heart, and you'll stand prepared for whatever evil your direction.

". . . and with your feet fitted with the readiness that comes from the gospel of peace."

Your feet are incredibly important as a soldier. Through the long and tiring campaigns ahead, through the marches, through the mud and mayhem, if your feet are fitted with deficient footwear, every step forward will be blistering grief. Have you ever noticed how improperly fitted footwear will throw the movement of your *entire* body into pitiful disorder? Disorder is not the will of any Commander-in-Chief for the forces he commands! The Bible confirms, **"For God is not a God of disorder but of peace"** (1 Corinthians 14:33).

The word *gospel* means "good news"—and our society is flooded with all sorts of new products, ideas, systems, and philosophies attached to a broadcast of how much good they can do us. But unless a thing establishes peace between our selves and our God, how much good does it do? Furthermore, we live in a society that so glorifies "bad news" that this is the news given both headlines and the bulk of media attention. This is despite the angst, despair, physical ailments, and cynicism "bad news" creates. However, the Good News that shods our feet us with peace only fits us when we walk in an accepting humility:

> **". . . since we are justified (acquitted, declared righteous, and given a right standing with God) through faith, let us [grasp the fact that we] have [the peace of reconciliation to hold and to enjoy] peace with God through our Lord Jesus Christ . . ."**
> **(Romans 5:1; The Amplified Bible)**

Unless we walk comfortably with the Good News of God's unmerited favor received by faith in Jesus—news that, when worn, brings sweet and supernatural comfort . . . we will never stand in readiness to make our charge against the darkness; instead, we'll find ourselves left behind in a Red Cross hospital, hobbled by our own resistance to the news of God's mercy toward us.

> **"In addition to all this, take up the shield of faith, with which you can extinguish all the flaming arrows of the evil one."**

Arrows are long-range weaponry—they strike you before it becomes apparent the enemy is even near. And because we know our enemy, we know the arrows he carries are carefully crafted shafts of FALSEHOOD tipped with arrowheads of piercing DECEIT. They fly swiftly, slicing the air with a whistle, and suddenly it's to late to raise your shield. Sometimes they are aflame so that even superficial contact ignites into a sud-

Inducted Into The Highest Military Assignment

den blaze—causing burns that take a long, long time to heal. Have you ever felt the heat of lying words?

> **"Like a madman shooting firebrands or deadly arrows is a man who deceives his neighbor and says, 'I was only joking!'"**
>
> **(Proverbs 26:18)**

> **"Like . . . a sharp arrow is the man who gives false testimony against his neighbors."**
>
> **(Proverbs 25:18)**

Arrows are perfect for ambushing a target—they do not sound off the exact position of the attacker as a rifle shot would; the loudest sound is sickening thump at the arrowhead's impact. That is to say, when a lie is lofted our way, we hardly ever know it's coming—and if it has been sailing awhile, it's nearly impossible to determine from whose mouth it originally took flight. But we do know the enemy who launched the shot—it is Satan who wants to pierce our hearts. So our lives depend on our shields.

Historically speaking, a shield is no frying pan-sized object. Properly positioned, many shields were designed to protect an area wider than the soldier's body, from the base of his neck down to his knees. A good soldier always kept the enemy in view . . . with his shield raised defensively in between. Caught in the path of an approaching rainfall of arrows, a soldier would crouch, plant the bottom of his shield into the ground, tilt it toward himself, and his whole body was protected.

Because this man-sized object was the first thing the enemy saw coming his way, it became the practice to emblazon across the front of the shield the warrior's "coat of arms"—the emblem which boldly signified to whom the soldier has pledged his life in allegiance. And this is the shield of every soldier of God: OUR LORD IS FAITHFUL TO HIS PROMISE TO SHIELD HIS PEOPLE FROM DESTRUCTION. And this is the "coat of arms" on every soldier's shield: THE NAME OF JESUS CHRIST. God has given us His Word that

> **". . . His truth *and* His faithfulness are a shield and a buckler. You shall not be afraid of the terror of the night, nor of the arrow (the evil plots and slanders of the wicked) that flies by day, nor of the**

pestilence that stalks in darkness, nor of the destruction *and* sudden death that surprise *and* lay waste at noonday. A thousand may fall at your side, and ten thousand at your right hand, but it shall not come near you."

(Psalm 91:4–7; The Amplified Bible)

Do you carry His faithfulness to you as your shield? Or do you attempt to enter the battles of any given day running ahead of His promises to you? To be honest, it is only the fact that His great shield of promises are ever before me, that allows my very small faith to protect it does. If not for the shield of His promises, surely we all would be overwhelmed! Walking apart from His promises has led to the moments of my greatest unfaithfulness. Let us equip ourselves with the truth of His undying devotion—His Word to us is our shield.

"Take the helmet of salvation . . ."

We, the followers of God have been saved from certain death. We have been saved from powerlessness. We have been saved from emptiness, aimlessness, and insignificance. But still we battle against our own fleshly desires; still we battle on behalf of those never been told of God's mercy; still we arm ourselves against a Devil who is out for blood. The fact that we must always walk with our helmets on to protect us in the battles as they come is evidence that stages of God's gift of mercy are being delivered to us with each new conquest. We've been enlisted to take possession of the final ground in the completion of His promised salvation. VICTORY IS LIFE! All soldiers, therefore, are challenged to . . .

". . . work out (cultivate, carry out to the goal, and fully complete) your own salvation with reverence *and* awe and trembling . . ."

(Philippians 2:12; The Amplified Bible)

1 Thessalonians 5:8 further clarifies that we wear **"the hope of salvation as a helmet."** We will encounter dangers we have yet to be delivered from—but we fight on with hearts full of the vision of victory. The hope of our salvation is our hold on this confidence: WE SHALL OVERCOME. The hope of our salvation, which has yet to be completed, is our hope against all the negative thoughts that may assail us. Our minds fixed on this hope protect against blows that would cause us to lose consciousness of our reason to endure. This hardship *shall* come to an end. Our helmets *shall* be put down . . . and replaced with victor's crowns.

> "Blessed is the man who perseveres under trial, because when he has stood the test, he will receive the crown of life that God has promised to those who love him."
>
> (James 1:12)

WEAPONS OF SALVATION

The Word of God is our sidearm in battle—it is loaded with Truth as we come against an enemy aiming to so rifle us with Falsehoods. The Word of God presents us with the truth of our sinfulness, God's supreme act of redemption at the cross, Jesus Christ the risen Savior and the righteous Kingdom coming to supersede all others. This is all the ammunition needed to drive Satan away again and again.

These truths will stand forever. Any situation, any circumstance, any power, any principle that draws its strength outside of God's word on the matter is temporal; as such, they remain subject to God's final Word. Read those words. Rehearse them. Old Testament words. New Testament words. Use them. Familiarize yourself with their application. Commit them to memory. Approach God repeating His own words of promise to us. Approach the enemy armed with God's words about his certain doom. Our enemy is outgunned; the Devil can never overpower us if we fight him with the Word of God. Jesus proved to be an expert marksman in the use of this weapon, as He defeated His enemy in a great desert battle.

Read the words of Matthew 4:1–11

The Voice of Praise is our long-range artillery—it pounds the enemy with explosions of our Faith, collapsing Satan's fortification before we even make contact as we storm its imposing walls. The Voice of Praise is no mere shout to rattle the enemy's confidence. A believer's outcry of praise is the advance cover needed to ram a stream of sunlight through the opposing darkness. Our voice of praise resonates and echoes the reassuring song of our enemy's defeat.

Our praise is given its trajectory by the heights to which we will extend our worship. Worship is when we raise up our lives as sacrifices offered to God in response to His mercy extended. The greater the trajectory of our worship, the loftier becomes our praise, the more stunning the resulting impact of our faith upon our circumstances. Our enemy's strength is breached; the Devil cannot slow the approach of his destruction. Joshua and the soldiers of ancient Israel demonstrated the efficiency of this weapon in their victory over Jericho.

Read the words of Joshua 5:13–6:27

The Act of Love is our hand-to-hand combat technique. It allows us to confidently sidestep our enemy's murderous lunges with carefully choreographed movements of Mercy. The Act of Love is the practice of directing our momentum away from where Satan wants to have us . . . preoccupied with ourselves, as sitting ducks. Instead, we move in response to the higher priority of another person's need suddenly in view. Our enemy is disoriented when his close-range jabs are not countered by reactionary acts of outrage and hostility . . . but rather are deflected off of our Love already in motion and up to speed. The Devil has no maneuver against swift compassion moving in unexpected directions. With this weapon, Jesus won a brilliant last second victory in the battle to save a lost man's soul.

Read the words of Luke 23:32–43

The Cry of Prayer is our air-strike capability—it is our beacon of Hope signaled to the Throne of Command, detailing the specific coordinates of enemy buildup in our vicinity, requesting intervention from the heavens ASAP (As Soon As Possible)! The Cry of Prayer is a plea for our superior technology to sweep over our position like a protective wing and crush all traces of satanic activity; a cascade of righteousness falls from the sky in response to the specifics of our need. Our enemy is stunned by the searing impact; the Devil has no choice but to count his losses. With this weapon, the prophet Elijah won the Battle of Mt. Carmel in spite of being apparently outnumbered.

Read the words of 1 Kings 18:16–40

Soldiers of the living God: *Use your weapons, or be held accountable for your ineffectiveness against the enemy!*

OUR ALLIES

". . . he will command his angels concerning you to guard you in all your ways; they will lift you up in their hands, so that you will not strike your foot against a stone . . . Because he loves me," says the LORD, "I will rescue him; I will protect him, for he acknowledges my name."

(Psalm 91:11–12,14)

You have powerful allies. You fight, and they fight along with you. You shout to Jesus the praise of victory, and they join their voices to the song. We alone call Jesus SAVIOR, but our allies have always known Him as HOLY, and they worship Him as well. While we sleep, they watch over our souls and our blessings, for they are not men that they should sleep. At God's command, they are at our side in a blur of light with weapons drawn on our behalf. They are not physical beings. They need not be visible. They are not bound by matter, or by space, or time. They are immortal. They are innumerable. They are warriors. They are nurses. They are conquerors. They are servants. They are *ANGELS*, "superior in might and power" (2 Peter 2:11; The Amplified Bible).

The born-again man or woman will become like Christ—humans do *NOT* become angels. Angels are an altogether different species of being, alien in lifestyle and language. But they are with us for the long haul.

"Are not all angels ministering spirits sent to serve those who will inherit salvation?"

(Hebrews 1:14)

This scripture confirms that angels have been given as our allies until our salvation is made complete—until the battles are no more and there is complete rest for God's people. But angels hostile to the plans of God are no longer ministering spirits; they have rebelled against a lifestyle of obedience to God and are useful only to the Devil. Like fallen Humanity, fallen angels have through and through become untrue to the blueprint for their existence. These demonic beings are followers of the archangel that stood highest and fell the farthest, Satan, who mounted a war against God, but **"was hurled to the earth, and his angels with him"** (Revelation 12:9).

Fortunately for us, as soldiers of the cross, friendly angels have pledged their allegiance to our Savior Christ. The Bible notes that right after Jesus won His great battle against Satan's temptation in the desert, angelic reinforcements flew to His side to support Him and attend to His needs. (Matthew 4:11) Indeed, Jesus was so matter-of-factly aware of the faithfulness and general battle-readiness of His beloved allies that, during His betrayal and arrest in the garden of Gethsemane, He sternly reprimanded the apostle Peter for brandishing and causing injury with a sword:

> **"Then Jesus said to him, 'Put your sword back into its place, for all who draw the sword will die by the sword. Do you suppose that I cannot appeal to my Father, and He will immediately provide Me with more than twelve legions [more than 80,000] of angels?'"**
> **(Matthew 26:52,53; The Amplified Bible)**

An important point is made here. Our otherworldly allies serve one Master, God alone. They respond to His voice, not ours. We do not pray to angels. When we call out for help, we must call out to God—it is *He* who dispatches angels to support us. With this understanding, help will be on its way even before you call, ". . . **for your Father knows what you need before you ask Him"** (Matthew 6:8).

Keep the faith, comrades! You need not see your supernatural allies to know that they encircle you in a protective hedge. Take to heart the example of the prophet Elisha and his servant on a day the woke up surrounded by hostile and ungodly men:

> "When the servant of the man of God got up and went out early the next morning, an army with horses and chariots had surrounded the city. "Oh, my lord, what shall we do?", the servant asked.
> "Don't be afraid," the prophet answered. "Those who are with us are more than those who are with them."
> And Elisha prayed, "O LORD, open his eyes so he may see." Then the LORD opened the servant's eyes, and he looked and saw the hills full of horses and chariots of fire all around Elisha."
>
> (2 Kings 6:15–17)

Our allies brighten the landscape with holy fire. God, our glorious fortress, towers above us. The refinement of our armor leaves nothing unprotected. The flash of our weaponry signals our righteous advance. Our Savior, in a spotless white cloak, personally spearheads our march. His double-edged sword is drawn. His face shines like the sun. What enemy should we fear? Who can accuse us of insignificance? We have been purchased from our past at the cost of a champion's blood, and have been brought over to the winning side!

> ". . . no weapon forged against you will prevail, and you will refute every tongue that accuses you. This is the heritage of the servants of the LORD . . ."
>
> (Isaiah 54:17)

STOP AND THINK.

I'm a soldier in the war to end all wars.
I've been inducted into the camp of righteousness,
and right makes might.
I pledge allegiance to Christ.
His victory is inevitable.
What enemy can fight back the right arm of God?

LIVE A LIFE WORTH GIVING.

PUBLIC SERVANTS

We/this delegation
wholly Thine
O divine Lord Christ,
born again
from above
now employed
at Your command:

that any refugee drifting into Your harbors
to be processed and legalized by Your love
that any immigrant once wretched
be re-created
old be gone
new citizenship given
all become candidates for important living

We/this delegation
wholly Yours
have been appointed to the public service
your Majesty confers
investing us with the weight
of speaking for the Heavenly State
that has adopted us as its very own

so that now we are known as ambassadors
traveling in the name of our LORD
appealing and imploring
for the end of rebellion
of anarchy
of isolation
and offering to all:

REUNION.

Chapter 11

Invested With The Highest Ranking Office

"... this is what the Lord says: 'If you repent, I will restore you that you may serve me; if you utter worthy, not worthless, words, you will be my spokesman.'"

(Jeremiah 15:19)

At some point in my early twenties, I finally learned the art to making friends of strangers—of entering the foreign territory of another man's life, yet returning unscathed, loaded with gifts and new resources. I learned to broadcast this simple message in whatever language most easily understood: "I AM FRIENDLY. I AM SAFE. YOU HAVE CAPTURED MY ATTENTION. AM I INVITED TO STAY?"

But even the best stated intentions are worthless unless our actions conform to our words. Trust always follows when truth comes through. I really was learning this; but my problem was my tendency to wander from my good intentions. I wandered from friendliness to selfishness, from safety to inscrutability, from attentiveness to intrusiveness. Instead of accepting the boundaries I was given, I took possession of unguarded territory without seeking permission.

As a result, some of the first friendships I initiated were also friendships I destroyed. I caused the breaks ... and the unnecessary pain. I did not understand diplomacy at first. But for the sake of lasting relations, I have finally caught on.

THE DIPLOMATS: A PARABLE

A confederacy of ruined nations cluttered the landscape on a planet known as Earth. They lived in isolation. A long forgotten union had been broken and these surviving nations were all that remained. As far as the eye could see, there was no clarity. Uncertainty darkened everyone's view. The peoples of these nations lived for only one purpose—to celebrate their independence. And shunning responsibility to a higher authority, all became subject to a stunning neglect of one another's needs. Then came the descent into ignorance.

Hysteria spread—the fear that life may end suddenly at any moment. And as individual after individual fell dead, there was constant panic on the unlit streets. Some succumbed to their illnesses; some were randomly massacred; others died by their own hands; all were wasted lives.

Famine ruled their bodies; shameless things ruled their souls. And on the outskirts of abandoned cities, stores of resources were deserted. Tanks of rust-tainted water leaked orange streams that stretched long into the starry nights. Forgotten granaries, broken open by time, exposed stale grain to mingle with wind-blown sand.

And then the strangers came. Envoys from another Kingdom.

Somehow, a place had been prepared for them in each of the nations before they had arrived. No one paid attention at first. The strangers called these gathering places by strange terms: *fellowships, congregations, assemblies, tabernacles*. But to the populace of the dying nations, the strangers were ambassadors of a Kingdom utterly foreign, and each gathering place, an embassy.

The ambassadors shared the outward appearance of the peoples, yet without any wounds . . . without disease. They explained to the peoples that they, too, were from the confederacy of nations. As they wandered at the brink of death, they began to cry for help and were rescued by a foreigner who called Himself a King. They were healed. They were adopted. They were appointed. And they were sent.

The first thing noticed was the light. And the clarity of vision. When an embassy opened, overcast clouds also opened to blue sky, and the dwellings of these ambassadors were flooded with unfamiliar light. Anyone curious enough to approach an Embassy was welcomed at the gate. If they asked for help, they were warmed with an embrace regardless of their ill condition. They were offered first aid under the auspices the King's hospitality. Shelter and asylum. Food and clean water. The opportunity to be saved. Acts of restoration. And then the ambassadors shared their King's appeal: REUNION.

Though the memory was distant and uncertain, it is revealed that the confederacy of nations once were all under the illustrious sovereignty of the King whom the ambassadors served. A long time ago, there was a rebellion; all authority was treated with contempt; the King's compassion was disdained and rejected; the privileges of citizenship were scorned. All that was left were dying embers of the glory that might have been. But so great was the heart of the King for His people, His desire was still for REUNION.

So He saved a few who were willing once again to pledge their allegiance—and those few he raised up to become His ambassadors. In their office of public service, they were sent out with supplies of water, food, and necessary aid. And they were furnished with the King's authority to establish corridors of His light to open paths out of the darkness.

Once this appeal was issued there were some who made the decision to enter the asylum of the embassy, pledge allegiance to the King, and disappear into the light. Most turned back to their dreary cities. And so it was until the day came when all the ambassadors were abruptly called home and the light of the embassies permanently extinguished. There was no announcement.

All who bowed in allegiance to the King were airlifted to a plateau above the uncertainty. Suddenly, visibility was endless, radiant, clear. The sun was everywhere in these rarified heights.

All who coveted their independence remained below in the ruins. Suddenly, the sun became visible to all within sight and all visibility became endless eruptions of solar fire, raging and cataclysmic, obliterating all shadows. The sun's fires swept down and purged through the nations below it.

FROM GOD TO HIS REPRESENTATIVES

"Each one should use whatever gift he has received to serve others, faithfully administering God's grace in its various forms. If anyone speaks, he should do it as one speaking the very words of God."
(1 Peter 4:10, 11)

Jesus Christ is called "KING OF KINGS AND LORD OF LORDS" (Revelation 19:16). It is my duty and my privilege to represent Him to the nations, if that were my calling—but representing Jesus to the people I'm closest to is a worthy enough task as it is. It is my duty to represent Him, because when He saved me, I took an oath of faithful citizenship and service to His holy Kingdom. It is my privilege, because my service is dependent on access to avenues of power reserved for royalty descended of God's holy bloodline! In all ways I have been included in that bloodline:

". . . you are no longer foreigners and aliens, but fellow citizens with God's people and members of God's household . . ."
(Ephesians 2:19)

It is important to reemphasize that this planet is not under the rule of the righteous standards that govern the citizens whose authority is God. LIFE, LIGHT, and LOVE do not rule here. Instead, all of Humanity's ways are legislated by DECOMPOSITION, DARKNESS, and DESECRATION. Satan holds dominion over all earthly affairs. Remember that Humanity once held the birthright to Earth and all Creation therein, but upon encountering Satan, human preeminence was handed away freely. God's wisdom was snubbed, His great faith in us disregarded. And the Devil is now in rental possession of the planet's real estate to set up an outlaw "government," independent of God, alien to Truth, subject to uncounted atrocities and unrestrained tyranny. Though God is sovereign over all of His Creation, for a brief time Satan has the "right" to roam the Earth.

Into this lawlessness, Christ has sent His ambassadors.

"Therefore, if anyone is in Christ, he is a new creation; the old has gone, the new has come! All this is from God who reconciled us to himself in Christ and gave us the ministry of reconciliation: that God was reconciling the world to himself in Christ, not counting men's sins against them. And he has committed to us the message of reconciliation. We are therefore Christ's ambassadors, as though God were making His appeal through us."

(2 Corinthians 5:17–20)

By original definition, an ambassador represents the person of his King. The King, of course, represents the embodiment of his Kingdom. Therefore, an ambassador's responsibility includes the proper representation of both the King and the Kingdom's people as a whole. The full title of this appointed office is "**ambassador extraordinary and plenipotentiary.**" The ambassador is defined as "extraordinary" because he uniquely represents his head of state. More revealing, we as the ambassadors of Christ are defined by the definition of the word "plenipotentiary": "*an envoy with full powers to take action or make decisions, etc., on behalf of the government he represents.*" (Oxford American Dictionary)

Know this: In your diplomatic service as Christ the King's personal ambassador, all the authority and the resources that are His have been placed at your disposal. You have the authority to access to the King at all times. You have the authority to voice His words. You have the authority to gain full disclosure on any matter related to the completion of your personal assignment. You have the authority to follow through on any work He's begun. You have the authority to confidently make decisions on the strength of your own reserves of wisdom and ask for extra supplies of any wisdom you are lacking. You have the authority to issue commands in His name, those based on the promises in His Holy Word. Your King has sent you out to stand in for Him and has equipped you with a documented authority by which to get the job done. Your King enforces and legitimizes that authority with all the power at His disposal.

> ". . . If anyone steadfastly believes in Me, he will himself be able to do the things that I do; and he will do even greater things than these, because I go the Father. And I will do [I Myself will grant] whatever you ask in My name . . ."
>
> (John 14:12, 13; The Amplified Bible)

The message Christ has given us to communicate has a supernatural effect. It is the "Good News" entrusted to Him when He walked the Earth as a man . . . the Holy Ambassador of mercy sent by a Sovereign God. When the message is received and embraced as the Truth, it produces not only new understanding—it goes on to produce new life.

Therefore, the success of our service mandates that we voice only the words God informs us to speak. The words of God anchor themselves as Truths, creating the structure for all growth—*our* words are merely expressions of a limited vocabulary. Jesus was so conscious of His limitations when He served in His office as a man, he said:

> ". . . I do not speak of my own accord, but the Father who sent me commanded me what to say and how to say it. I know that his command leads to eternal life. So whatever I say is just what the Father has told me to say."
>
> (John 12:49, 50)

Though our words by themselves cannot convey the gift of life, the success of our service will not be in ourselves, but in our *authority* to convey the command of our God.

Jesus pioneered the ministry of reconciliation. But He didn't just lay the groundwork—He became the foundation for the renewal of friendly relations between God and all those made in God's image. As ambassadors we must be confident and assured in all we do to continue the work passed on to us.

According to the *Encyclopedia Americana*, "An ambassador is charged with four basic responsibilities that ranking diplomats have carried throughout history. These are: *protection of his country's interests abroad; reporting to his government on conditions in the country of his assignment; negotiation of agreement; ceremonial representation.*"

PROTECTION OF HIS OR HER COUNTRY'S INTERESTS

The resources of our Kingdom are rich with supernatural concentrations of LIFE, LIGHT, and LOVE. The interests of our Kingdom are served as we labor to open the "iron curtain of darkness," to introduce our Kingdom's surplus of resources. Our job includes utilizing all channels of diplomacy to generate acceptance for our King's foreign policy: *emergency relief in exchange for coming under the protectorship of His jurisdiction.*

Unfortunately, most of the peoples behind the "curtain" are taught that it's better to die than to give up independence—antithetical to our new life of free-will obedience and allegiance. Yet, in spite of suspicion, opposition, even open hostility, the art of our diplomacy is persistent. By definition, the best diplomat is honest in his or her determination to seek and build upon common interests as a basis for mutual agreement. A person may be taught it is better to die than to submit, but that doesn't make it true. *Everyone* is interested in being *truly* better off. If it can be demonstrated that a relationship with our King increases one's standard of living, then the word will spread on its own. The Gospel will run. Evangelism will result. And the Kingdom's interests will be promoted.

REPORTING TO HIS OR HER GOVERNMENT

The next basic responsibility of an ambassador is communication—constant back-and-forth between King and ambassador such that he or she who represents the King is of one mind with the desires and intentions of the King. Prayer is our direct and private line through which we learn the King's desires.

The ambassador becomes the channel of authorized input as to where the King should direct special attention or special relief. Specifics must be relayed. Because of the authority delegated to any ambassador, the King must clearly communicate a response: either YES . . . NO . . . or, sometimes, WAIT. This is one of the reasons our God expects *us* to pray if we expect *Him* to move; only in situations of dire absence of wisdom does any Sovereign insert Himself directly into current foreign affairs without being *invited* by acknowledged diplomatic channels. Such moves are made without fanfare. The standards of diplomacy dictate that no kingdom imposes its will upon another, lest it be greeted with contempt. In this universe, free-will choices are sacred.

As ambassadors of Christ, it must be made evident to all that our allegiance and the support we depend on are not of this world. When it is clear that the flow of God's intercessory power is held in reserve and is initiated only by our prayer—only then will the foreigners who surround us recognize that our King is principled, benevolent, and fair to all who call upon him.

NEGOTIATION OF AGREEMENT

The *Encyclopedia Americana* states that, "**In order for there to be negotiation, there must be difference of values or national interest on the one hand, and on the other, some interests common to all parties.**"

With whom are we to negotiate? The question is easily answered when we recognize who it is that negotiates with us, drawing us into agreements, pacts, and alliances on the basis of our common interests. Who else, but our neighbor? Humankind negotiates with humankind. But if the common interests are self-centered, the result of the negotiations will be self-serving. The negotiations might hard-boil down to this:

> "**Come along with us; let's lie in wait for someone's blood, let's waylay some harmless soul; let's swallow them alive, like the grave, and whole, like those who go down to the pit; we will get all sorts of valuable things and fill our houses with plunder; throw in your lot with us, and we will share a common purse**"
>
> (**Proverbs 1:11–14**)

Fortunately, we are no longer self-serving—now we serve the King. But if we are now new creatures in Christ, do we still share enough in common with those who remain alien to the Kingdom of God? Let's not kid ourselves—all of Humanity shares the unique heritage of being made by God, for God, in the image of God. All of us are filled with the seeds of godlikeness. All of us are lost and meaningless without God. Together we are the reason for the Cross of Christ. Together we have been offered mercy and a second chance to be friends with God.

Still, there is a difference in interests to be negotiated; when the light became a fixture within us, it put us at odds with the surrounding darkness. The two cannot coexist in equanimity; either the fire goes out and the darkness remains, or the dawn arrives to dispel the night.

What proposal then do we bring to the table as ambassadors? We bring the proposal that there is no reason we all can't be brought into the light; that since the light has been promised to become our new Day, there is no reason that anyone should escape its warmth against our cold flesh.

What spirit do we bring to these negotiations? We bring the spirit that is the glory of our King—a spirit willing to sacrifice itself so that another might be saved. A spirit able to echo the wisdom of an ambassador known as Paul:

> "Though I am free and belong to no man, I make myself a slave to everyone, to win as many as possible. To the Jews I became like a Jew, to win the Jews. To those under the law I became like one under the law (though I myself am not under the law), so as to win those under the law. To those not having the law I became like one not having the law (though I am not free from God's law but am under Christ's law), so as to win those not having the law. To the weak I became weak, to win the weak. I have become all things to all men so that by all possible means I might save some. I do all this for the gospel, that I might share in its blessings."
>
> (1 Corinthians 9:19–23)

Negotiation is a common ability among men and women, but as diplomats of the highest rank we must learn to excel at it. It must become our particular occupation and our peculiar artistry. If one takes a look at Christ and His life-saving negotiations as described in the gospels, *it is clear that as He extended God's gift of reconciliation. He never approached two people the same way.* A good negotiator will perceive the needs presented to him from "across the table," and in a bold leap of creativity will appropriately adapt his presentation of the King's offer to meet that need. This is the legacy of public service practiced by Christ and passed on to us. We are assured the Kingdom's full support in this service. With our King at our rear, who can topple our efforts? What we do in His name will surely endure.

CEREMONIAL REPRESENTATION

The embassy is our church, our congregation, our common fellowship. Wherever the King's ambassadors assemble themselves, a little land is cleared upon which the Kingdom we celebrate as our home is magnified and applauded. The embassy is our beloved home away from home.

> ". . . I would rather be a doorkeeper in the house of my God than dwell in the tents of the wicked."
>
> (Psalm 84:10)

All who enter through the gates do so in acknowledgement of our King; yet, all who are foreign to our ways *must* be welcome to visit. Our embassies must be located for all to see—they are the places that bear witness of our allegiance to an overcoming Authority. If there are walls, they must be hung with the best that our Kingdom has to offer. The uniqueness of our people is to be exhibited; the power of our King is to be exalted. The safety, the majesty, the thanksgiving, the diversity, the privileges of our citizenship must all be on display. But even without walls or roof, a caring COMMUNITY must be firmly in place.

As far as the authorities of this dark world are concerned, wherever Christ's ambassadors dwell, those embassy grounds are His Kingdom's soil. Transgression by any hostile authority is an act of spiritual warfare. Ambassadors enjoy "diplomatic immunity" from the threat of indictment and condemnation by the dark powers that reign over lands separated from righteousness. Those enlisted in the King's service, the King Himself has committed to protect.

"Do not touch my anointed ones; do my prophets no harm."

(1 Chronicles 16:22)

"In righteousness you will be established: Tyranny will be far from you; you will have nothing to fear. Terror will be far removed; it will not come near you."

(Isaiah 54:14)

Whether by a warming fire or beacon searchlight, an embassy *must* bring a change to the darkness. It is the light that draws the curious to seek and to find; it is the light that lends color and depth to life once barely visible; it is the light that overcomes uncertainty, reawakening graying senses; it is the light that rouses and recreates a world.

But what happens when the light is allowed to grow dim? Or is shut off to save the extra expense? What happens when our Kingdom's representation goes untended? What would the King say? I believe the King might say something like this:

"Church, what are you doing? You who are My ambassadors, the keepers of My embassies, the legacy of My foreign mission . . . why is my work in ruins? Why have you suffocated the flame? Why have you quenched My Spirit's lamp? Color has turned to neutrality; brightness to twilight; magnificence to mediocrity. Instead of search and discovery, there is routine and ritual—your artistry in displaying my glory has been smothered."

We eat. We sit in the air conditioning. We relax. We disintegrate into factions, denominations, and divisions. We get comfortable. We entertain ourselves. We perform the minimum requirements. We offer our leftovers. We fluff our pillows at night. We sacrifice NOTHING.

As the candlewicks burn out, we lounge beside the pool. The grounds overgrow with weeds. The private telephone line rings in the upper room—we are not around to answer. Our King leaves a message that goes unheard. We have broken the oath of service.

At the comfort of the poolside we build a private bungalow, paint it real nice and say to ourselves, "I'm a Catholic/ Apostolic/ Baptist/ Nazarene/ Protestant/ Lutheran/ Pentecostal/ Methodist/ Unitarian/ Presbyterian/ Episcopalian/ etc. . . . and this is *my* house." We add a little crystal and perhaps call it a cathedral. But what becomes of the mission we were authorized to complete? What becomes of our public service assignment as an ambassador? What becomes of our responsibility to our embassy to represent our *Kingdom* . . . *not* our own preferences and tastes?

> "'Is it a time for you yourselves to be living in paneled houses, while this house remains a ruin?' Now this is what the LORD Almighty says: 'Give careful thought to your ways. You have planted much, but have harvested little. You eat, but never have enough. You drink, but never have your fill. You put on clothes, but are not warm. You earn wages, but only to put them in a purse with holes in it.'
>
> This is what the LORD Almighty says: 'Give careful thought to your ways. Go up into the mountains and bring down timber and build the house, so that I might take pleasure in it and be honored,' says the LORD. 'You expected much, but see, it turned out to be little. What you brought home, I blew away. Why?' declares the LORD Almighty. 'Because of my house, which remains a ruin, while each of you is busy with his own house.'"
>
> (Haggai 1: 4–9)

When the personal idiosyncrasies and inclinations of any ambassadorial staff are built up to a higher priority than the simple delivery of the King's message of compassion, that embassy will find its support cut off. Faithfully translating the King's message is the only hard work that is rewarded; not self-service. An ambassador who departs the saving intent of His King leaves himself bereft of the King's support. How traitorous to play it safe within our own ceremonial constructs and traditions—instead of daring to follow through on the King's day-to-day plans, crafted in His own blood to bridge day-to-day needs. As the only source of foreign aid those standing outside the embassy gates will ever see, when we abandon our call to serve the people's needs, we are no longer fit to be called the King's representatives.

Warnings From A King To His Ambassadors

A fool danced alone on a mountaintop.
He danced with the wind.
His heart stopped.
He fell.

Ambassador, you exalt yourself and call yourself out as though on a mountaintop above the morality of all others. But you grasp at the wind, for you are self-important and do the work of Satan against me. You do not gather, you scatter. You reward yourself and give me nothing. I will take life away from you, for you have been selfish stewards with the many gifts I have given. You will fall and be brought down.

Man in the glare of your headlights
stops your car on a highway in the night
waving you on to turn your vehicle around
with grand sweeping arm motions
tossing out sparkling dust
sweetly persuading you with his smiling teeth
to turn back and go in the wrong direction.

Ambassador, Satan stands before you, beckoning you to lose all sense of direction in this present darkness as he sprinkles before you shiny, distracting things. He smiles as you satisfy his desire by self-reliantly taking your eyes off the road just ahead of you; your heart turns to things that fasten your attention, but are too insignificant to hold on to, and, by tomorrow, are all blown away. You will crash and burn by the roadside.

On a gravelly field
with his back against the rising sun
a fool juggles three stones
standing still
all day.

Ambassador, you stand still as a fixture on a doomed horizon. There is no fruit in your hands. No good thing have you labored into being. You have never cleared the land or even offered to pick up a hoe or plow. You lazy, useless servant! You miss the sunrise as it rises behind you, your eyes caught within your own moving shadow. You fix your attention on self-indulgent futility, spinning lifeless things around in your hands. You add nothing to my Kingdom. The field I have given you to work remains a barren waste because you concentrate your attention on things that don't matter. You have given me nothing. You will receive no reward.

STOP AND THINK.

I am a high-ranking representative in the government of God.
I have been clothed in His robes of righteousness.
I have been given the King's authority.
I have been sent on a mission of mercy.

While I remain in this strange land:

I will display my King's glory,
I will communicate His words,
and with as many as will receive Him
I will negotiate the go-ahead for my King to send His aid.

LIVE A LIFE WORTH GIVING.

MEDICAL MIRACLE

I am free of my disorders
I will never ail again
I've been injected with a Righteousness
to overcome my Sin

fatal symptoms have weakened,
I am stronger now
than I ever before have been.

I've received a holy vaccination
tapped from Jesus' veins;
untainted blood poured out one day
on a cross soaked red on a hill far away

the transfusion was successful
yesterday I was dying,
today my life is saved.

My Physician has finished His operation
I'm no longer listed in critical condition
my systems all have stabilized
a balance has been attained
He's transferred me to Recovery
He says vital signs are normal as far as He sees
He's written out a new prescription for me
I'm spiritually fit to go home now.

My Physician monitors my therapy
giving regular doses of mercy to me
so that Rehabilitation is a certainty.

He has deleted my medical history.

Jesus tells me, "The emergency is over."
and I do believe
I can finally get through this night in peace.

Chapter 12

Full Recovery

"Do not be overcome by evil, but overcome evil with good."

(Romans 12:21)

I wish I could run as fast and freely as a cat darts through the grass. But my feet aren't normal; these days they generate far more discomfort than speed. My podiatrist says they're as flat as a pancake, which is no news to me. I've always had flat feet. My mother has them too; I inherited them from her side of the family.

After approximately fifty years of walking this earth, Ma's feet began to cause her such sudden piercing pains, she'd be hobbled in her tracks—able to stay on her feet only from the sheer necessity to turn back home. She was reduced to walking to work with a cane. Sometimes she would leave for work, and on the way to the subway the pain nearly crippled her. Ma would be forced to turn right back around and spend the day in bed; the unexpected pains were quickly becoming debilitating. But, praise to God who answers prayer, the problem was alleviated when Ma was prescribed orthopedic inserts for her shoes—specially molded to fit her feet and compensate for their imperfections.

After over *thirty* years pounding about on this earth, my imperfect feet are failing me, too. A barely perceptible arch is visible, but only when I stand high on my toes. Just standing barefoot washing the dishes, my feet have been causing increasing amounts of pain. My podiatrist only took a glance at my pancaked feet in action before prescribing specially molded orthopedic inserts for *my* shoes, as well. I'm aware that unless I wear them, the joints of my feet will continue to deform underneath my weight, and the pain will only worsen. I have accepted the expense of corrective measures.

It's funny to remember now. I was in a store once purchasing a pair of shoes, and the salesman attending me commented that I had the worst pair of fallen arches he had ever seen. I reacted defensively, with a picture of archaeological ruins flashing through my mind. With a touch of naive pride, I told the salesman that he was very much mistaken—nothing had fallen in these particular feet, because my feet never had any arches to begin with!

In other words, from the beginning, my feet had never been normal.

NORMAL RESPONSES

Before we receive Christ, the life we live is not the life a human being was designed to live. It is like a child born with a hole in its heart . . . a "blue baby" . . . born dying, with an anemic blue flesh tone, because of a faulty pump and the consequent lack of oxygen to enrich the blood. Our entire condition is ABNORMAL.

Starting with the spirit of each man and woman, everyone is born with a birth defect . . . a terminal condition . . . like a bird born without wings, a horse born without legs, a tree with no leaves, or a land with no rain.

> **"As for you, you were dead in your transgressions and sins, in which you used to live . . ."**
>
> **(Ephesians 2:1, 2)**

Like a caterpillar out of sync with its own lofty blueprint, each of us entered the world doomed to flounder in the mud, unaware that we must one day *transform* to suit the sky. Oh, we *want* to fly. We try everything from hang gliding to parachuting to space shuttling—yet in and of ourselves, we possess no wings. We sense that we belong somewhere in the heights. We try desperately to climb up mountain peaks, up corporate ladders, above our own personal bests, or on the backs of those we exploit. So why is it that the eagle soars so easily above us all, majestic over everything it surveys? What are we missing?

> "Then God said, 'Let us make man in our image, in our likeness, and let them rule over the fish of the sea and the birds of the air, over the livestock, over all the earth, and over all the creatures that move along the ground.' So God created man in his own image, in the image of God he created him; male and female he created them."
> (Genesis 1:26, 27)

The image, the reflection, the unique likeness of God . . . in quality, in character, and in holy context . . . has from the very beginning been Humanity's intended NORM. Normal for you. Normal for me. God made *Himself* the Standard by which we each were engineered, and the Law by which we were to be governed. But a random agent of lawlessness, Satan, was allowed access into our original system (like a computer virus scrambling a perfectly programmed database). Any new input we received was immediately garbled; all existing principles broke down into gibberish; everything we produced came out hopelessly distorted.

I must reemphasize, before we receive Christ, we are out of order—without Christ ordering our lives, intended laws of operation do not apply.

Though we are programmed to be "the image of God," we do not naturally operate according to God's guiding principles. God cannot die. God cannot lie. God cannot change. God cannot fail. Yet all these things we *naturally* do.

The supernatural internal principles, genetically encoded, that guide our development in the womb so that we are born as human beings and not pigs or ostriches—these internal principles have been unsoundly reintegrated. Yes, for the most part we still physically resemble the perfectly good human beings God first created—*but resemblance is as far as it goes*. Our natural-born spirit is unstable; it has no integrity. Spiritual principles are bypassed. Guidance systems are short-circuited. Buffers against the invasion of random and unholy variances are entirely disengaged.

So complete is our separation from intended laws, the quality, the character, and the original holy context of human life have been subject to uncontrolled mutations. Everything is affected. Hence, spiritual monstrosities have been born amongst us and are labeled "deviants," "psychos," or "maniacs." Social disturbances, physical diseases, and natural disasters run amok through our world. Babies continue to be born, or stillborn, with meaningless deformities.

Nothing that is of this world is certain. Seasons disappear; our greatest loves cause us pain; our theories turn out to be incomplete; our joys plummet to newer lows; our marriages break up; our "civilizations" fall; friends can't always be trusted; our desires consume us; we become slaves to our own leisurely pursuits; our time slips away; our success doesn't satisfy; fame makes us crazy; our wealth is left behind to be redistributed amongst those who never knew us. None of this makes any sense.

With nothing as it should be, true-to-form humans are no longer found on the Earth—only billions of spiritual/emotional/physical variants and vagaries here today and gone tomorrow. This was our lot until Christ entered into the equation.

"Jesus Christ is the same yesterday and today and forever."
(Hebrews 13:8)

Jesus Christ has been eternally established as the refabricated design for Humankind. His quality, His character, and His context in perfect holiness have become a design replacement for what Humanity has permanently lost. Jesus did not fail. Jesus will not change. Jesus has never lied. Jesus is still alive. *JESUS HAS BEEN GIVEN TO BECOME OUR NORM . . . THE REFORMULATED STANDARD OF QUALITY, CHARACTER, AND HOLY LIVING.* No one gets any better.

Jesus Christ is revolutionary design breakthrough—*everything will be measured against Him, and because He cannot vary, all judgments are verifiable and final*. Now each of us has a right to choose to let the revolution pass us by. Those who choose to remain as is will die as is expected. However, those who choose to conform to Christ will be upgraded to a quality of living out of this world! This is God's plan for salvaging those who would choose to live life the way He meant it to be lived:

> "For those whom He foreknew [of whom He was aware and loved beforehand], He also destined from the beginning [foreordaining them] to be molded into the image of His Son [and share inwardly His likeness], that He might become the firstborn among many brethren."
>
> (Romans 8:29; The Amplified Bible)

A GENETIC INHERITANCE RELEASED

God purposely made us. We are no accident or happenstance. God, the Creator of all kinds of life, decided to reproduce His own kind. Whatever God speaks comes into being—and when He spoke of Himself, humans resulted.

The Amplified Bible reminds us "**God is a Spirit (a spiritual Being)**" **(John 4:24)**. Made as we are in His image, we are also His direct spiritual offshoots. Every attribute He owns, every glorious trait, everything that resembles His very appearance is passed along in each human being's genetic blueprint. And even though Humanity is infected with sin that dooms each of His offshoots to a spiritual death, there are dormant seeds of His Being reproduced and clustered deep inside the darkest reaches of all that is dead within us.

But those of us who have gladly received an infilling of all that Christ is have been supernaturally born again. We are revived. We are once again exposed to the holiness of God. The germs of holiness built into the mysteries of our molecular structure are now awakened. They are packed with the spiritual imprint of God; if planted and nurtured in the proper ground, the reawakened seeds of His "image" we possess are certain to sprout a crop of life indistinguishable from that of God. We would blossom as a "species" of God. Never gods in and of ourselves, but simple offshoots of God. Branches of the Vine. Sharing the stature of God. Flourishing as does God. As enduring as God. Having the fragrance of God. Arrayed with the beauty of God. Bearing the abundant, life-giving fruit of our God. But before the seeds of His "image" can fully flower within us, a greatly-awaited event must first take place.

> "Beloved, we are [even here and] now God's children; it is not yet disclosed (made clear) what we shall be [hereafter], but we know that when He comes *and* is manifested, we shall [as God's children] resemble *and* be like Him, for we shall see Him just as He [really] is. . ."
>
> (1 John 3:2; The Amplified Bible)

Jesus Christ did not attain His full glory while the seeds of His Godhood were still planted in mortal flesh; he needed an undying, unlimited, resurrected body, brilliant in holy purity. For that same reason, He is coming again to collect all who are right now being conformed into His glorious likeness. He is coming to "replant" us into a new form of clay—so that we too may rise into being as He now is.

Our contact with sin has leeched human flesh of the quality originally instilled at Creation. The bodies we now have are no more than the dust, blown into memory by time—they are unfit for the seeds of godlikeness burst forth in the full glory of their beauty. The seeds within us are of eternal stuff; they spring up in their fullness only in the rich sustenance of immortality.

> "And just as we have borne the likeness of the earthly man, so shall we bear the likeness of the man from heaven. I declare to you, brothers, that flesh and blood cannot inherit the kingdom of God, nor does the perishable inherit the imperishable . . . for the trumpet will sound, the dead will be raised imperishable, and we will be changed. For the perishable must clothe itself with the imperishable, and the mortal with immortality."
>
> (1 Corinthians 15:49–50, 52, 53)

God has built a time clock into all things. Animals, insects, and flowers instinctually respond to the time of day, to the seasons, to the count of the years. Glaciers and rocks and trees record the passage of centuries. Even the planets orbit like clockwork. Seeds are no different; if a garden planted with a particular type of seed is cultivated properly—if watered well, and warmed by the sun—all that take root will shoot up blossoms at exactly the same time. There will be a harvest of newness, a potpourri of idyllic pleasures.

God is a Master Gardener. He is mercifully nurturing us to a fully reawakened life by the gentle touch of His hand. He's not finished with us yet. With compassion, He has saturated our lives with the refreshment of His Spirit. All that is now needed to release the full splendor of the intended immortality implanted in our cells, is for that trumpeted moment when time ceases to matter, and we who await His coming are irradiated in the warmth of the Son's welcoming face.

"He has made everything beautiful in its time. He has also set eternity in the hearts of men . . ."

(Ecclesiastes 3:11)

FINAL STATEMENT

We have caught sight of His mercy. We have beheld the purpose of our living. We have glimpsed a glory not yet fully revealed.

Clarity is especially important to me, but very difficult to achieve. In conversation, in thought, or in vision. I am a portrait artist. For years I've found myself drawn to the challenge of taking either the photograph or the reality of an individual sitting before me and reconstructing the vision I perceive. What I will eventually render is not exactly as it appears. Change is inherent in the process of the translation to paper or canvas. But, for me, the changes wrought in the process are a necessary, clarifying achievement.

I believe that all humans are as limited in their understanding as Paul has described to us in the book of 1 Corinthians 13:12, where we are portrayed as perceiving as through a darkened sheet of glass or a distorted reflection in a mirror.

I, however, am a portrait artist and I must struggle to see in spite of these limitations. My favorite method is to begin with a black & white photograph of the subject. In so doing, I begin my search for clarity as through a cloak of varying grays. My understanding begins with nothing but a sketch. Clarity is constructed layer by layer. From which direction is the light cast? At what point will I notice and repair my initial misalignments? Nostrils too wide. An ear lobe too low. The left eyebrow arched at too acute an angle. Then, a skin color is invented, or rather, a mixture of disparate light and dark colors. Then I add gradations, ever-softened gradations, blended and combined. It all comes to life in the process of clarifying. And my eye is always enthralled by the rising vision.

In the end, my portraits never seem to me to be finished. Perhaps that is because God's re-creation of my life is yet an unfinished thing . . . a promised thing. I repeat—God is not done with me yet—nor you. In His hands we are masterpieces nearing completion. Can you see yourself, His handiwork, more clearly now?

Our falsehoods and doubts are finally overcome in the sweetness of a clarified vision.

> **"Where there is no vision [no redemptive revelation of God], the people perish . . ."**
>
> **(Proverbs 29:18; The Amplified Bible)**

STOP AND THINK.

To say good-bye to myself as I used to be
is the fulfillment of my spiritual destiny;
shedding the hindrances in which I have crawled,
unfolding wings of unspeakable glory, so that I might now arise.
All my ills are thrown aside
for the good that's now settled in its place.

AND I LIVE A LIFE WORTH GIVING.

About the Author

James Haywood Rolling, Jr., a native of the borough of Brooklyn in New York, is a fine artist and art educator currently completing his doctoral degree in education at Teachers College, Columbia University. He has already earned a Master of Fine Arts degree in the visual arts from Syracuse University, and a Master of Education from Teachers College. He also works as the Director of Academic Administration for the Department of Curriculum and Teaching at Teachers College.

Mr. Rolling has been a member of the Brooklyn Tabernacle for over fifteen years. Beginning with his ministry as a young teens Sunday Bible Hour teacher, he has served in several ministries in his congregation over the years and is currently a member of the Grammy Award-winning Brooklyn Tabernacle Choir. He and his wife, Me'Shae, live in New York City.

To order additional copies of

Living
Sacrifices

Have your credit card ready and call:

1-877-421-READ (7323)

or please visit our web site at
www.pleasantword.com

Also available at: www.amazon.com

Printed in the United States
30194LVS00005B/73-510